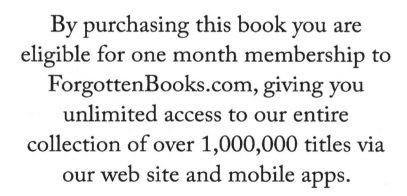

ISBN 978-0-331-76168-9
PIBN 11055646

For support please visit www.forgottenbooks.com

Compliments of

R. A. MAXWELL,

State Treasurer.

ANNUAL REPORT

OF THE

STATE TREASURER

FOR THE

Fiscal Year ending September 30, 1884.

TRANSMITTED TO THE LEGISLATURE, JANUARY 7, 1885.

ALBANY, N. Y.:

WEED, PARSONS & COMPANY, PRINTERS.

1885.

STATE OF NEW YORK.

No. 3.

IN SENATE,

JANUARY 7, 1885.

ANNUAL REPORT

OF THE TREASURER FOR THE FISCAL YEAR ENDING
SEPTEMBER 30, 1884.

STATE OF NEW YORK:
TREASURER'S OFFICE,
ALBANY, *January 7*, 1885.

Hon. D. McCARTHY, *President pro tem. of the Senate :*

Herewith I transmit my annual report for the fiscal year ending
September 30, 1884.

Respectfully yours,

R. A. MAXWELL,
Treasurer.

REPORT.

STATE OF NEW YORK:

TREASURER'S OFFICE,
ALBANY, *January 7*, 1885.

To the Legislature:

Pursuant to the requirements of law, I submit my annual report, giving a summary of receipts and disbursements from the several funds during the fiscal year commencing October 1, 1883, and ending September 30, 1884. I also give a statement showing the condition of the treasury on the 1st day of January, 1885.

R. A. MAXWELL,

Treasurer.

ANNUAL REPORT OF THE TREASURER.

CONDITION OF THE TREASURY ON THE MORNING OF JANUARY 1, 1885.

Balance in treasury October 1, 1884......		$3,167,825 71
Receipts during October	$112,178 76	
Receipts during November	183,686 14	
Receipts during December...............	120,122 80	415,987 70
		$3,583,813 41
Payments during October................	$618,776 77	
Payments during November..............	381,733 98	
Payments during December	691,242 32	
		$1,691,753 07
Balance in treasury January 1, 1885..............		$1,892,060 34

RECEIPTS.

GENERAL FUND.

State tax	$6,143,636 65
Salt duties	73,518 12
Auction duties.....................................	22,673 29
Peddler's license	65 00
Interest on Treasurer's deposits....................	39,680 39
From insurance companies for expenses of Insurance Department.....................................	86,056 68
Bank Department...................................	20,058 78
Game and fish protectors	311 59
New Capitol, sale of old material	3,525 00
Stationery sold by Comptroller	975 65
* Tax on corporations	1,603,612 75
Notaries' fees......................................	314 16
Asylum for Insane Criminals........................	1,905 35
Public administrators	10,429 38
War claims..	54,946 52
Fees, Secretary of State	18,280 87
Fees, Clerk Court of Appeals........................	2,561 50
Fees, Comptroller..................................	1,011 30
Fees, Railroad Commission..........................	32 35
Sales of general fund land..........................	9,296 34
Grants of land under water	5,222 25
Rent of land	20 00

Contributions from Gas-light Companies.

Albany Gas-light Co.....................	$16 33
Albion Gas-light Co.....................	2 61
Auburn Gas-light Co....................	6 53
Brooklyn Gas-light Co..................	130 64
Binghamton Gas-light Co................	3 26
Brockport Gas-light Co.................	1 63
Buffalo Mutual Gas-light Co............	48 99
Buffalo Gas-light Co...................	32 66
Batavia Gas-light Co...................	2 12
Corning Gas-light Co....	59
College Point Gas-light Co.............	65
Citizens' Gas-light Co.............. ..	17 20
Citizens' (Brooklyn) Gas-light Co..........	78 38
Citizens' (Warsaw) Gas-light Co...........	1 00
Citizens' (Rochester) Gas-light Co.........	25 00
Citizens' (Buffalo) Gas-light Co...........	19 59

*For detailed statements of amounts received from corporations, page 54.

Citizens' (Poughkeepsie) Gas-light Co......	$33 38
Central Gas-light Co......,..........	29 07
Canandaigua Gas-light Co...............	3 26
Cohoes Gas-light Co....................	3 26
Coney Island Gas-light Co...............	20 69
Chuctanunda Gas-light Co...............	3 26
Consumers' Gas-light Co.................	13 06
Dansville Gas-light Co..................	1 63
Elmira Gas-light Co....................	3 26
East River Gas-light Co.................	3 01
East Chester Gas-light Co...............	3 26
East Albany Gas-light Co...............	3 26
Flatbush Gas-light Co..................	3 59
Fulton Gas-light Co....................	3 23
Fishkill and Matteawan Gas-light Co.......	1 30
Flushing Gas-light Co..................	2 74
Fulton Municipal Gas-light Co............	128 67
Geneva Gas-light Co...................	2 37
Geneseo Gas-light Co..................	1 04
Gas-light Co. of Syracuse...............	21 55
Glens Falls Gas-light Co................	2 29
Harlem Gas-light Co...................	117 58
Hoosick Falls Gas-light Co..............	4 02
Hempstead Gas-light Co.................	1 63
Hudson Gas-light Co...................	3 26
Homer and Cortland Gas-light Co..........	3 26
Ithaca Gas-light Co....	4 73
Ilion and Mohawk Gas-light Co...........	6 01
Jamaica Gas-light Co...................	5 34
Johnstown Gas-light Co.................	1 15
Jamestown Gas-light Co.................	4 24
Knickerbocker Gas-light Co..............	97 98
Lyons Gas-light Co....................	84
Little Falls Gas-light Co................	1 57
Lockport Gas-light Co..................	2 61
Le Roy Gas-light Co...................	1 63
Malone Gas-light Co...................	1 27
Minden Gas-light Co...................	69
Metropolitan Gas-light Co..........	163 30
Middletown Gas-light Co...............	1 31
Manhattan Gas-light Co................	261 28
Metropolitan (Brooklyn) Gas-light Co......	56 82
Municipal (N. Y.) Gas-light Co	195 96
Norwich Gas-light Co	78
New York Mutual Gas-light Co	228 62
New York Gas-light Co........	261 28
Nassau Gas-light Co...................	65 32
Niagara Falls Gas-light Co..............	4 13
Northern Gas-light Co.................	8 16
Oneida Gas-light Co...................	1 16
Oswego Gas-light Co...................	6 63

Owego Gas-light Co......................	$3 09
Palmyra Gas-light Co	1 31
Poughkeepsie Gas-light Co................	5 49
People's (Albany) Gas-light Co	3 26
Port Jervis Gas-light Co..................	1 31
Peekskill Gas-light Co...................	2 02
Penn Yan Gas-light Co...................	1 62
People's (Brooklyn) Gas-light Co.........	65 32
People's (Albany) Gas-light Co., by H. Q. Hawley, receiver................	7 63
Port Henry Gas-light Co..................	44
Rome Gas-light Co.......................	2 29
Rhinebeck Gas-light Co	52
Rochester Gas-light Co	39 19
Rondout and Kingston Gas-light Co........	4 24
Richmond County (Stapleton) Gas-light Co.	22 77
Saratoga Gas-light Co	2 61
Saugerties Gas-light Co...................	2 09
Sing Sing Gas-light Co	1 47
Schenectady Gas-light Co.................	6 53
Troy Gas-light Co.......................	19 60
Tarrytown and Irvington Gas-light Co	6 53
Union (E. N. Y.) Gas-light Co............	4 90
Utica Gas-light Co.......................	5 23
Waverly Gas-light Co	3 26
White Plains Gas-light Co	1 63
Watertown Gas-light Co	6 53
Williamsburgh Gas-light Co...............	65 32
Whitehall Gas-light Co...................	1 31
West Troy Gas-light Co	3 26
Yonkers Gas-light Co	19 60

$2,497 29

Contributions from Railroad Companies.

Auburn & Owasco Lake R. R. Co..........	$6 26
Amsterdam Street R. R. Co...............	7 21
Adirondack R. R. Co.....................	209 21
Atlantic Avenue (Brooklyn) R. R. Co......	276 93
Albany Railway Co	84 72
Addison & Northern Penn. R. R. Co.......	33 88
Bath & Hammondsport R. R. Co..........	19 22
Bradford, Eldred & Cuba R. R. Co........	240 43
Bushwick R. R. Co	182 20
Buffalo Street R. R. Co..................	32 98
Buffalo East Side R. R. Co	12 04
Broadway (Brooklyn) R. R. Co............	241 83
Buffalo Lehigh R. R. Co.................	47
Brooklyn & Rockaway Beach R. R. Co.....	17 83
Buffalo, New York & Phil. R. R. Co.......	1,717 40
Buffalo, Pittsburgh & Western R. R. Co....	102 08
Brooklyn City R. R. Co	860 42
Boston, Hoosac Tunnel & Western R. R. Co.	307 53

2

Brooklyn, Bath & Coney Island R. R. Co...	$31 72
Broadway & Seventh Ave. R. R. Co........	436 25
Brooklyn City & Newtown R. R. Co........	125 67
Buffalo Creek R. R. Co	45 72
Boston & Albany R. R. Co................	762 92
Brooklyn Crosstown R. R. Co	109 25
Brooklyn, Flatbush & Coney Island R. R. Co.	50 34
Buffalo Creek Transfer R. R. Co.....	3 56
Buffalo Erie Basin R. R. Co..............	80
Binghamton & Port Dickinson R. R. Co....	18 04
Conesus Lake R. R. Co..................	7 17
Cazenovia, Canastota & De Ruyter R. R. Co..	64 00
Chemung R. R. Co......................	43 97
Central Crosstown R. R. Co..............	48 66
Corning, Cowanesque & Antrim R. R. Co...	68 50
Chateaugay R. R. Co....................	12 84
Coney Island Elevated R. R. Co..........	5 47
Central City R. R. Co..................	23 52
Cooperstown & Susquehanna Valley R. R. Co.	5 25
Clove Branch R. R. Co..................	29 30
Catskill Mountain R. R. Co..............	51 62
Central Park, North & East River R. R. Co.	431 05
Coney Island & Brooklyn R. R. Co........	173 30
Christopher & Tenth Street R. R. Co......	98 27
City R. R. Co. of Poughkeepsie	14 44
Coney Island, Sheepshead Bay & Ocean Avenue	
R. R. Co............................	7 70
Chateaugay Ore & Iron R. R. Co	110 82
Connecting Terminal R. R. Co...........	13 16
Cortland & Homer R. R. Co.............	9 90
Delaware, Lackawanna & Western R. R. Co.	1,707 15
Dunkirk & Fredonia R. R. Co....	18 72
Dunkirk, Allegheny Val. & Pittsb'h R. R. Co.	162 81
D. & H. C. Co. acct. Alb. & Susq. R. R. Co..	1,223 08
D. & H. C. Co. acct. N. Y. & Canada R. R. Co.	582 71
D. & H. C. Co. acct. Rens. & Saratoga R. R. Co.	730 00
D. & H. C. Co. acct. U., C. & B. R. R. Co..	160 80
D. & H. C. Co. acct. Rome & Clinton R. R. Co.	4 55
Dry Dock, East Broadway & Battery R. R. Co.	577 81
Elmira & Horseheads R. R. Co	13 54
East Genesee St. & Seward Avenue R. R. Co.	10 30
Elmira & Williamsport R. R. Co...........	14 49
Elmira, Jefferson & Canandaigua R. R. Co..	95 62
Eighth Avenue R. R. Co.................	439 60
Fonda & Fultonville R. R. Co............	5 78
Forty-second Street, Manhattanville & St.	
Nicholas Avenue R. R. Co..............	2 22
Frankfort & Ilion R. R. Co.............	8 84
Forty-second St. & Grand St. R. R. Co......	292 68
Fifth Ward R. R. Co....................	11 71
Fonda, Johnstown & Gloversville R. R. Co..	184 40
Greenwich & Johnsonville R. R. Co........	4 39
Grand St., Prospect Park & Flatbush R. R. Co.	32 63

Grand St. & Newtown R. R. Co............	$14 04
Genesee & Water Street R. R. Co..........	2 30
Greenwich & Johnstown R. R. Co..........	47 23
Hartford, Connecticut & Western R. R. Co..	178 53
Herkimer, Newport & Poland R. R. Co.....	76 36
Houston, West St. & Pavonia Ferry R. R. Co.	28 02
Harlem Bridge, Morrisania&Fordham R.R. Co.	45 45
Herkimer & Mohawk R. R. Co............	7 94
Ithaca, Auburn & Western R. R. Co........	3 38
Jerome Park R. R. Co....................	8 55
Jamaica & Brooklyn Horse R. R. Co.......	1 38
Johnstown, Gloversville & Kingsboro R.R. Co.	17 33
Jamaica & Brooklyn Road R. R. Co........	19 98
Kingston City R. R. Co..................	25 97
Kaaterskill R. R. Co....................	33 31
Lebanon Springs R. R. Co................	72 65
Lehigh & Hudson River R. R. Co..........	19 33
Lehigh Valley, acct. Geneva & Ithaca R. R. Co.	460 77
Lake Champlain & Moriah R. R. Co.......	111 71
Lackawanna & Pittsburgh R. R. Co........	16 83
Lake Shore & Michigan Southern R. R. Co..	769 14
Long Beach Marine R. R. Co.............	4 69
Long Island R. R. Co	2,322 84
Lake Ontario & Southern R. R. Co.........	6 09
Manhattan R. R. Co.....................	3,013 89
Middletown & Crawford R. R. Co..........	15 79
Mohawk & Ilion R. R. Co................	58
Marine Railway Co.......	5 54
Middleburgh & Schoharie R. R. Co........	20 54
Manhattan Beach R. R. Co..............	36 90
Middletown, Unionville & Water Gap R.R. Co.	42 03
N. Y. Central & Hudson River R. R. Co....	23,938 23
N. Y., Lake Erie & Western R. R. Co......	3,544 22
N. Y., Lackawanna & Western R. R. Co....	37 81
North Second St. & Middle Village R. R. Co.	7 81
New Brighton & Onondaga R. R. Co.......	8 40
N. Y. City, New Haven & Hartford R. R. Co.	452 53
N. Y. City & Northern R. R. Co	213 95
N. Y., Woodhaven & Rockaway R. R. Co...	83 18
N. Y. & New England R. R. Co...........	129 34
Ninth Avenue R. R. Co.................	45 55
N. Y. & Sea Beach R. R. Co.............	40 15
Northern Central R. R. Co..............	79 19
N. Y., Susquehanna & Western R. R. Co...	5 99
New Jersey & New York R. R. Co........	15 15
New York & Harlem R. R. Co............	482 88
New Williamsburgh & Flatbush R. R. Co...	16 72
Newburgh, Dutchess & Connecticut R. R. Co.	214 12
N. Y., Ontario & Western R. R. Co........	130 66
N. Y., Pennsylvania & Ohio R. R. Co......	62 06
N. Y. & Manhattan Beach R. R. Co........	5 13
N. Y., West Shore & Buffalo R. R. Co.....	1,173 57

N. Y., Chicago & St. Louis R. R. Co..	$224 69
Northern Central R. R. Co. for Elmira & Williamsport R. R. Co..................	41 38
North. Cent. R. R. Co. for Chem'g R. R. Co.	97 35
Northern Central R. R. Co. for Elmira, Jefferson & Canandaigua R. R. Co..........	241 83
Northern R. R. Co........................	39 83
Niagara Falls & Susp. Bridge R. R. Co.....	9 90
Olean Street R. R. Co....................	7 61
Ogdensburg & Lake Champlain R. R. Co...	480 62
Prospect Park & Coney Island R. R. Co....	101 20
Prospect Park & Flatbush R. R. Co........	1 84
Port Dickinson & Chenango River R. R. Co.	2 91
Port Jervis & Monticello R. R. Co.........	85 20
Poughkeepsie, Hartford & Boston R. R. Co.	218 19
Rome & Clinton R. R. Co.................	33 88
Rochester City & Brighton R. R. Co........	139 84
Rome, Watertown & Ogdensburg R. R. Co..	1,582 18
Rochester & Lake Ontario R. R. Co........	50 58
Rochester & Pittsburgh R. R. Co..,........	583 84
Sterling Mountain R. R. Co...............	5 74
Southfield Branch R. R. Co...............	40
Syracuse, Chenango & New York R. R. Co..	11 86
Sodus Bay & Southern R. R. Co...........	5 00
Syracuse, Genesee & Corning R. R. Co.....	67 94
Sixth Avenue R. R. Co....................	386 66
South Brooklyn Central R. R. Co..........	35 60
Syracuse, Binghamton & N. Y. R. R. Co....	142 22
South Ferry R. R. Co....................	12 51
Syracuse & Onondaga R. R. Co............	27 13
Staten Island Shore R. R. Co..............	2 40
Springfield & Sardinia R. R. Co............	18 78
Syracuse & Geddes R. R. Co.............	5 46
Staten Island R. R. Co...................	179 37
Stoney Clove & Catskill Mountains R. R. Co.	57 94
Schoharie Valley R. R. Co...............	15 66
Skaneateles R. R. Co....................	26 21
Second Avenue R. R. Co..................	371 30
Silver Lake R. R. Co....................	23 00
Southern Central R. R. Co...............	679 40
Saratoga, Mt. McGregor & L. George R. R. Co.	34 84
Steinway & Hunter's Point R. R. Co.......	23 71
Susquehanna Valley R. R. Co..............	51 64
Syracuse & Binghamton R. R. Co..........	791 47
Syracuse, Geneva & Corning R. R. Co......	329 30
Syracuse, Ontario & New York R. R. Co...	147 51
Troy & Lansingburgh R. R. Co....	207 80
Troy & Boston R. R. Co..............	251 12
Tonawanda Valley & Cuba R. R. Co........	258 56
Third Avenue R. R. Co..................	827 29
Twenty-third Street R. R. Co..............	209 32
Tioga & Elmira State Line R. R. Co........	8 07

Troy & Albia R. R. Co..................	$17 44	
Tioga R. R. Co......................	51 54	
Utica, Ithaca & Elmira R. R. Co.........	105 13	
Utica, Clinton & Bingh'ton (Horse) R. R. Co.	47 36	
Ulster & Delaware R. R. Co.............	295 05	
Utica & Black River R. R. Co..........	912 40	
Utica & Mohawk R. R. Co..............	68	
Van Brunt Street & Erie Basin R. R. Co..	19 08	
Washington St. & State Asylum R. R. Co.	16 70	
Walkill Valley R. R. Co.	129 06	
Watervliet Turnpike R. R. Co...........	36 26	
Williamsburgh & Flatbush R. R. Co......	28 90	
		$62,373 18

County Taxes.

Arrears....................	$63,874 17	
Interest.............................	14,656 49	
Redemption	124,387 97	
Tax sales...........	53,816 35	
Advertising	43 80	
		256,778 78

State Prisons.

Sing Sing............................	$238,179 56	
Auburn..............................	115,408 09	
Clinton............................. ...	46,899 74	
		400,487 39

Transfers:

From Common School Fund, capital for bonds received by State Engineer and Surveyor for General Fund lands sold per chap. 260, Laws of 1835............   2,932 75

Miscellaneous.

Copying Historical Records..............	$6 00
For trespass, etc., on State lands..........	3,907 49
Chateaugay Ore and Iron Co., one year's lease of the Plattsburgh & Dannemora R. R..............................	1 00
Clerk of Senate, unexpended balance.....	342 87
Clerk of Assembly, unexpended balance...	20 00
Satisfaction of judgment, State vs. W. H. Bloomingdale, etc....................	688 99
Comptroller, sundry amounts............	122 32
Clerk of Assembly, amount returned same advanced on account contingent expenses,	750 00
Costs of cancellation of tax sales, etc.....	101 98
Agent and Warden Clinton Prison, unexpended balance of appropriation for roofing................................	418 20

Daniel S. Lamont, Private Secretary to
Governor, collections from U. S. land
sales.................................. $6,961 89
Fines for selling adulterated milk........ 148 80
                                     $13,479 54

Total receipts credited General Fund..... ....$8,836,683 11

COMMON SCHOOL FUND.

Bonds for lands, principal................ $17,093 70
Bonds for lands, interest................ 4,137 99
Rent School Fund land................. 24 59
Bonds for loans, principal............... 4,000 00
Bonds for loans, interest................ 308 00
Loan of 1840, principal................. 2,750 00
Loan of 1840, interest................. 1,686 45
Interest on U. S. bonds, 4 per cent, 1907.. 90,020 00
Interest on Albany county bonds......... 3,925 00
Interest on Albany City Hall bonds...... 5,405 00
Interest on New York city bonds........ 37,150 00
Interest on Middletown bonds........... 2,120 00
Interest on District of Columbia bonds ... 12,775 00
Dividends on Manhattan Company's stock. 4,000 00
                             $185,395 73

   Transfers:
From U. S. Deposit Fund....... .... $100,000 00
From U. S. Deposit Fund............... 27,056 73
From General Fund for capital of said
Fund, chap. 520. Laws 1883........... 2,000 00
From General Fund for revenue of Com-
mon School Fund, chap. 382, Laws 1849 1,012 46
                            130,069 19

Total receipts credited Common School Fund...... $315,464 92

ELMIRA FEMALE COLLEGE EDUCATIONAL FUND.

Interest U. S. bonds, 4 per cent, 1907..... $180 00
Interest New York city bonds........... 315 00
Capital received for Oswego bonds 6,000 00
Interest received on Oswego bonds 962 50
   Transfer:
From General Fund for revenue of Elmira
Female College Educational Fund for
interest 301 03

Total receipts credited Elmira Female Col. Ed. Fund. $7,758 53

COLLEGE LAND SCRIP FUND.

Interest on U. S. bonds.....	$8,472 00
Interest on Albany city bonds	350 00
Interest on State stock	1,716 00
Interest on Buffalo city park bonds	2,590 00
Interest on District of Columbia bonds	3,102 50
Interest on Albany county bonds	2,150 00
Interest on deposits	857 21

Total receipts credited College Land Scrip Fund... $19,237 71

LITERATURE FUND.

Interest on U. S. bonds, 4 per cent, 1907...	$400 00
Interest on U. S. bonds, 4½ per cent, 1891.	4,617 00
Interest on State stock	7,800 00
Interest on Dist. Col. bonds	912 50
Albany Insurance Co. dividends	400 00
Transfers:	
From U. S. Deposit Fund	28,000 00
From General Fund for interest	9 52

Total receipts credited Literature Fund $42,139 02

MILITARY RECORD FUND.

Interest on Albany city bonds	$2,100 00
Interest on Buffalo city park bonds	630 00
Interest on deposits	100 27

Total receipts credited Military Record Fund $2,830 27

UNITED STATES DEPOSIT FUND.

Loans of capital	$155,274 59
Loans of capital interest	125,919 20
Rent of U. S. Deposit Fund land	197 00
Sales of U. S. Deposit Fund land	678 18
Interest on Dist. of Col. bonds	18,797 50
Interest on U. S. bonds, 4 per cent	30,040 00
Interest on Troy city bonds	1,750 00
Interest on State stock	3,120 00
Transfers:	
From General Fund for interest	3,520 82
From revenue to the capital of U. S. Deposit Fund, per chapter 150, Laws 1837, for premises bid in for the State in 1883, etc	4,500 00

From General Fund for failure of title.... $300 00
From General Fund for loss on sales .:....   950 50

Total receipts credited U. S. Deposit Fund....... $245,047 79

FREE SCHOOL FUND.

On Account of School Tax.

Albany county	$82,481 47
Allegany county	13,419 13
Broome county	16,042 82
Cattaraugus county	15,847 52
Cayuga county	29,376 67
Chautauqua county	24,512 25
Chemung county	16,735 83
Chenango county	17,674 36
Clinton county	9,569 95
Columbia county	30,821 77
Cortland county	10,136 60
Delaware county	12,959 66
Dutchess county	47,269 29
Erie county	101,002 96
Essex county	10,275 22
Franklin county	7,809 77
Fulton county	7,277 91
Genesee county	20,257 40
Greene county	12,306 72
Hamilton county	933 04
Herkimer county	21,868 89
Jefferson county	23,881 72
Kings county	303,002 68
Lewis county	8,906 55
Livingston county	22,389 40
Madison county	18,443 89
Monroe county	68,588 59
Montgomery county	21,425 11
New York county	1,410,988 73
Niagara county	23,389 39
Oneida county	52,464 69
Onondaga county	56,661 73
Ontario county	26,589 81
Orange county	41,433 24
Orleans county	13,500 54
Oswego county	22,317 46
Otsego county	20,185 37
Putnam county	7,471 47
Queens county	43,613 51
Rensselaer county	47,954 69
Richmond county	11,612 84
Rockland county	12,949 06
St. Lawrence county	23,225 95

Saratoga county.........................	$21,257 58	
Schenectady county.....................	11,367 33	
Schoharie county	10,582 54	
Schuyler county	6,774 78	
Seneca county	14,143 31	
Steuben county........................	21,025 71	
Suffolk county.........................	16,858 61	
Sullivan county........................	5,337 90	
Tioga county........	11,017 09	
Tompkins county......................	14,151 62	
Ulster county	22,676 40	
Warren county	5,512 26	
Washington county	22,605 78	
Wayne county..........................	24,332 07	
Westchester county	78,660 07	
Wyoming county	13,493 44	
Yates county..........................	11,045 51	
		$3,100,437 65
Erroneous apportionment to town of Colesville, Broome county, refunded........	$45 54	
Interest on deposits	3,829 99	
		3,875 53

Total receipts credited Free School Fund.........$3,104,313 18

CANAL FUND.

Interest U. S. 4 per cent bonds	$51,800 00	
Interest U. S. 4½ cer cent bonds	32,175 00	
Taxes	2,947,108 35	
Interest on deposits	15,178 50	
Balance account, Canal Commissioner....	433 33	
Balance accounts, Canal Superintendents .	136 63	
Balance accounts, engineers	55 47	
Use of dredge.........................	6,287 39	
Sale of materials, etc...................	433 94	
Sale of ice permits.....................	1,391 96	
Sale of abandoned lands	5,352 94	
Rent of surplus water	770 00	
Deposits of contractors	9,135 00	
Fees....................................	343 86	
Errors of collectors' accounts	1 71	
Tolls of 1882..........................	6 54	
Towing sunken boat	78 50	

Total receipts credited Canal Fund.............$3,070,689 12

RECAPITULATION OF FUND RECEIPTS.

General Fund	$8,836,683 11
Common School Fund......	315,464 92

3

College Land Scrip Fund $19,237 71
Elmira Female College Educational Fund,   ·7,758 53
Literature Fund 42,139 02
Military Record Fund..................   2,830 27
United States Deposit Fund 345,047 79
Free School Fund......................   3,104,313 18
Canal Fund 3,070,689 12

    Total receipts ....:....................$15,744,163 65

PAYMENTS.

Executive Department.

Grover Cleveland, Governor, salary	$10,000 00	
David B. Hill, Lieutenant-Governor, salary,	5,000 00	
Daniel S. Lamont, private secretary, salary,	4,000 00	

Clerk Hire.

Goodwin Brown	$1,800 00	
William G. Rice	1,500 00	
Thomas Newcomb	1,500 00	
Irving F. Cragin	1,500 00	
	6,300 00	
Charles A. Earl, messenger	1,200 00	
Incidental expenses	2,134 05	
Governor's mansion	2,144 31	
Apprehension of criminals	321 20	
		$31,099 56

Secretary of State's Office.

Joseph B. Carr, Secretary of State, salary,	$5,000 00	
Anson S. Wood, Deputy Secretary of State, salary	4,000 00	

Clerk Hire.

Lee Chamberlain	$2,500 00	
Tiras H. Ferris	1,800 00	
Will G. Carr	1,650 00	
A. D. W. Strickland	1,600 00	
David Caswell	1,600 00	
H. A. Cozzens	1,600 00	
W. H. Stevens	1,725 00	
David J. Blauvelt	1,500 00	
W. E. Kisselburgh, Jr	1,500 00	
L. Herdman	1,500 00	
L. L. Olmsted	1,500 00	
C. H. Hyde	1,200 00	
	19,675 00	
Geo. H. Overocker, messenger	1,000 00	
Incidental expenses	2,257 25	
		31,932 25

Comptroller's Office.

Alfred C. Chapin, Comptroller, salary.......	$4,500 00
Ira Davenport, late Comptroller, salary.....	1,500 00
Thomas E. Benedict, Deputy Comp., salary..	2,849 46
Henry Gallien. late Deputy Comp., salary...	1,096 77

Clerk Hire.

Sidney W. Park.................	$2,400 00
George Seeley................	2,200 00
Willis E. Merriman............	2,200 00
Beverly F. Cole	1,048 28
F. N. Chase..................	1,700 00
John J. Walsh................	765 52
Marcus B. Williams	1,425 00
George W. Bliss..............	1,537 50
W. H. Van Allen..............	1,537 50
M. A. Nalley	617 82
A. Cartwright................	1,350 00
Prine Cavert	569 90
William K. Brown	617 82
*Frank H. Brandon	275 84
*M. G. Graham...............	505 00
*F. B. Holderidge.............	333 34
*O. V. B. Taylor.............	301 08
*W. H. Sanger...............	425 00
†John R. Powers.............	11 49

Late Clerks.

Le Grand Benedict............	916 66	
Thomas H. Schuyler	668 10	
George W. Cocks...	651 72	
G. D. Ferris.................	250 00	
C. W. Campbell.............	455 17	
J. W. Shelley................	555 17	
		23,317 91
Messenger service		786 39
Incidental expenses.......................		3,436 28

$37 486 81

State Treasurer's Office.

Robert A. Maxwell, State Treasurer, salary..	$5,000 00
Edgar K. Apgar, Dep. State Treasurer, salary,	4,000 00

Clerk Hire.

Richard G. Milks.......	$3,000 00	
Philo H. Backus................	2,200 00	
James H. Schooley............	2,000 00	
Frederick V. Booth	2,000 00	
William C. Hackney...........	1,000 00	
Samuel V. B. Swan.............	120 00	
		10,320 00

*Balance of salary paid from appropriation for Expenses of Public Lands.
†Balance of salary paid from appropriation for Bureau of Canal Affairs.

Samuel V. B. Swan, messenger............ $1,000 00
Incidental expenses....... ....   885 12
                                          ────────── $21,205 12

Attorney-General's Office.

D. O'Brien, Attorney-General, salary....... $3,750 00
Leslie W. Russell, late Att'y-Gen'l, salary... 1,250 00
Isaac H. Maynard, Deputy Att'y-Gen'l, salary, 3,000 00
Wm. A. Poste, Deputy Att'y-Gen'l, salary... 3,000 00
J. A. Dennison, late Dep. Att'y-Gen'l, salary, 1,000 00
J. C. Keeler, late Deputy Att'y-Gen'l, salary, 1,000 00

Clerk Hire.

E. G. Whitaker................ $1,566 66
C. R. Hall.................... 1,375 00
Byron Traver................. 1,350 00
J. H. Hogan.................. 1,375 00
F. B. Delehanty 1,200 00
E. A. Bedell................. 1,050 00
W. R. De Lano...............   900 00
M. H. Quirk..................   933 34
W. M. Thomas................ 1,433 32

Late Clerks.

J. C. Winslow................   550 00
W. C. Percy..................   550 00
G. W. Wright 550 00
P. R. McMonagle.............   550 00
M. W. Nolan.................   366 66
B. F. Willson 400 00
                              ────────── 14,149 98
Costs of suits............................   8,169 22
Expenses and disbursements...............   6,094 48
                                          ──────────   41,413 68

State Engineer and Surveyor's Office.

Elnathan Sweet, Eng. and Sur., salary....... $3,750 00
Silas Seymour, late Eng. and Sur., salary... 1,250 00
Charles Hilton, Deputy Eng. and Sur., salary, 3,000 00
R. L. Fox, late Deputy Eng. and Sur., salary, 1,000 00

Clerk Hire.

John P. Masterson............. $1,312 50
Charles D. Burrus............. 1,687 50

Late Clerk.

Silas Seymour, Jr.............   500 00
                              ──────────   3,500 00
Incidental expenses...................... 1,636 71
                                          ──────────   14,136 71

Department of Public Instruction.

William B. Ruggles, Sup't, salary..........	$5,000 00
James E. Morrison, Deputy Sup't, salary....	3,500 00

Clerk Hire.

Charles V. Hooper..............	$2,400 00
George B. Weaver..............	2,000 00
James E. Kirk................	1,500 00
Albert Cornwall................	1,320 00
Wm. J. Kernan................	1,000 00
John D. Moon.................	640 00
	8,860 00
Messenger's service	360 00
Superintendent's expenses................	170 64
Incidental expenses......................	2,469 59
	$20,360 23

Insurance Department.

John A. McCall, Jr., Superintendent, salary,	$7,000 00
Michael Shannon, Deputy Supt., salary.....	4,500 00

Clerk Hire.

M. H. Robertson..............	$4,075 00
John S. Patterson..............	2,500 00
H. J. Haynesworth.............	2,362 50
John G. Clifford..............	2,000 00
James E. Cross................	1,800 00
George T. Harvey..............	1,800 00
William H. McCall.............	1,725 00
Isaac Vanderpoel..............	1,800 00
H. D. Appleton................	1,500 00
John A. Horan.................	2,375 00
M. A. Nolan..................	1,425 00
R. L. Wetmore....	1,200 00
J. O. Baldwin.................	1,200 00
Nathaniel Hyatt...............	1,200 00
Alex. Clarke..................	1,200 00
C. R. De Freest...............	1,311 58
J. H. G. Connell..............	900 00
Fred. T. Van Hoesen....... ...	846 62
M. B. Osborne................	980 00
Thomas J. Baunon.............	1,193 33

Late Clerks.

A. U. Jacobs................ ...	748 39
Charles H. Barber..............	153 32
H. P. Royals.....	300 00
	34,595 74
T. F. Behan, messenger.................	665 00

Postage................................ $719 70
Expenses of examination, etc.............   4,434 84
Printing.................................   5,829 25
Incidental expenses.....................   1,428 41
                                           —————— $59,172 94

Bank Department.

Willis S. Paine, Superintendent, salary.... $5,000 00
J. Van Vranken, Deputy Supt., salary......   2,708 33

Clerk Hire.

E. A. Werner.................. $1,830 00
L. F. Cahill..................   1,540 00
                               ——————
                                              3,370 00
J. D. Moriarity, messenger................   371 65
Postage........ ....   316 44
Incidental expenses......................   2,432 18
Expenses of examining banks.............   4,174 73
                                           ——————   18,373 33

Clerk of Court of Appeals.

E. O. Perrin, Clerk of Court, salary........ $5,000 00
W. H. Shankland, Deputy Clerk of Court,
    salary...............................   3,000 00

Clerk Hire.

Gorham Parks................. $2,167 99
Richard M. Barber..............   1,500 00
Guy E. Baker..................   1,500 00
                               ——————
                                              5,167 99
William Honig, messenger................   866 68
Crier and attendants.....................   8,099 46
Stenographer.............................   800 00
Incidental expenses 1,664 72
                                           ——————   24,598 85

State Reporter.

Hiram E. Sickles, Reporter, salary.......... $5,000 00
Peyton F. Miller; Clerk, salary.............   2,000 00
                                           ——————   7,000 00

Regents of the University.

David Murray, Secretary, salary.......:... $3,500 00
D. J. Pratt, late Asst. Secretary, salary.....   1,899 99
C. F. Peck, Botanist, salary 1,500 00
Incidental expenses......................   3,893 82
                                           ——————   10,793 81

State Library.

H. A. Homes, Librarian	$2,500 00	
S. B. Griswold, Librarian	2,000 00	
Geo. R. Howell, Librarian	1,780 00	
J. R. Boynton, Librarian	1,300 00	
H. E. Griswold, Librarian	900 00	
D. V. R. Johnson, Librarian	855 00	
Berthold Fernow, Clerk	1,500 00	
Library expenses	2,350 58	
Binding	1,688 20	
Purchase of books	4,793 12	
Clinton manuscripts	3,400 00	
Subject-index catalogue	1,196 76	
		$24,263 66

New Capitol.*

Interest on award for land	$600 00	
Labor account, construction	747,104 03	
Materials, etc., account, construction	558,721 27	
		1,306,425 30

State Museum Natural History.

James Hall, Curator, salary	$3,500 00	
James Hall, Geologist, salary	2,500 00	
Assistants	2,424 98	
Drawings	2,996 24	
Increase and preservation of collections	2,613 54	
Printing and engraving	10,462 51	
Sundry expenses	3,469 67	
Joseph A. Lintner, Entomologist	2,000 00	
		29,966 94

National Guard.

Adjutant-General's Department	$30,444 94	
Inspector-General's Department	6,211 28	
Commissary-General's Department	185,425 95	
Paymaster-General's Department	44,310 00	
Inspector-General Rifle Practice	15,096 69	
Judge-Advocate-Gen'l and Courts of Inquiry,	2,505 47	
Head-quarter expenses	8,743 08	
Military Fund Apportionment	89,428 00	
Arsenals and armories, maintenance, repairs, etc.	111,014 46	
		493,179 87

War Claims.

Investigating and settling claims	2,615 64

*For detailed statement of expenditures for New Capitol for fiscal year ending September 30, 1884, see page 77.

Commissioners of Public Charities.

Charles S. Hoyt, Secretary, salary..........	$3,500 00	
James O. Fanning, Asst. Secretary, salary...	2,500 00	
Expenses of Secretary and Commissioners...	2,747 18	
Office expenses, etc......................	4,547 97	
Support, transportation, care, treatment, and cost of removal of alien and State paupers.	36,286 17	
		$49,581 32

State Board of Health.

Alfred L. Carroll, Secretary, salary.........	$1,893 71	
Elisha Harris, late Secretary, salary	1,166 66	
Expenses of members of the Board.........	1,108 46	
Clerks and messenger....................	8,834 62	
Experts, etc.............................	3,836 26	
Postage and incidental expenses...........	5,795 81	
		22,635 52

Bureau of Labor Statistics.

Charles F. Peck, Commissioner, salary......	$2,702 88	
David Healey, Clerk, salary..............	1,524 75	
Extra clerk hire, traveling and office expenses	2,862 57	
		7,090 20

Civil Service Commission.

Augustus Schoonmaker, Comm'r, salary....	$1,833 34	
Henry Richmond, Comm'r, salary..........	2,000 01	
John Jay, Comm'r, salary	1,333 33	
Silas W. Burt, Chief Examiner, salary	3,600 00	
C. B. Angel, Secretary, salary.............	583 34	
J. A. Betts, late Secretary, salary	416 66	
Messenger...............................	250 00	
Stenographer............................	508 09	
Postage.................................	230 00	
Incidental expenses......................	1,607 13	
Expenses of Commissioners ......:......	1,433 76	
Expenses of Chief Examiner.............	535 75	
		14,331 41

Board of Claims.

Henry F. Allen, Commissioner, salary......:	$6,666 67	
George M. Beebe, Commissioner, salary.....	6,666 67	
Lyman H. Northrup, Commissioner, salary ..	6,666 67	
Edwin M. Holbrook, Secretary, salary......	3,165 39	
F. G. Jewett, stenographer, salary..:......	1,979 17	
W. E. Young, clerk, salary....	1,307 99	
Office expenses, etc...............	5,505 59	
		31,958 15

Railroad Commission.

John D. Kernan, Commissioner, salary...	$8,000 00	
William E. Rogers, Commissioner, salary..	8,000 00	
John O'Donnell, Commissioner, salary....	8,000 00	
William C. Hudson, Secretary, salary.....	3,000 00	
T. B. O'Neil, Marshal, salary...........	1,500 00	
John D. Kernan, Commissioner, expenses..	573 23	
William E. Rogers, Commissioner, expenses	331 85	
John O'Donnell, Commissioner, expenses...	537 34	
Postage.........................	400 00	
Experts, clerks and stenographer..........	12,304 20	
Office and other expenses...............	23,578 75	
		$66,225 37

Legislature.

Pay of officers and members.............		$331,727 83	
For contingent expenses.			
Clerk of Senate..............	$4,500 00		
Clerk of Assembly...........	11,808 58		
		16,308 58	
Witnesses and committees............ ...		759 64	
Postage.....................		3,767 98	
Manuals		2,133 31	
Transportation....................		3,773 47	
Miscellaneous......................		11,120 16	
Investigations......................		51,257 32	
			420,848 29

Superintendent of State Prison.

Isaac V. Baker, Superintendent, salary....	$6,000 00	
Isaac V. Baker, Superintendent, expenses.	212 77	
Clerk hire.............................	1,375 00	
Messenger and office expenses...........	710 18	
		8,297 95

Sing Sing Prison.

Maintenance.......	$176,366 59	
Repairs, etc	15,500 00	
		191,866 59

Auburn Prison.

Maintenance.........................	$113,048 42	
Repairs and water............	7,575 00	
		120,623 42

Clinton Prison.

Maintenance	$100,002 93	
Repairs, etc	20,372 17	
		120,375 1

Agent for Discharged Convicts.

H. L. Arnold, Agent, salary	$2,500 00	
H. L. Arnold, Agent, expenses, etc.......	5,000 00	
		7,500 00
Transportation of convicts......................		12,909 24

Court of Appeals.

William C. Ruger, Judge, salary	$9,500 00	
Charles Andrews, Judge, salary..	9,000 00	
Robert Earl, Judge, salary	9,000 00	
Theodore Miller, Judge, salary..........	9,000 00	
George F. Danforth, Judge, salary.......	9,000 00	
Francis M. Finch, Judge, salary.........	9,000 00	
Charles A. Rapallo, Judge, salary........	9,000 00	
	$63,500 00	
Reports sent to other States.	204 80	
Court of Appeals Libraries.............	2,930 00	
		$66,634 80

State Assessors.

John L. Williams, Assessor, salary.......		$2,499 96	
J. D. Ellis, Assessor, salary		2,500 00	
S. N. Wood, Assessor, salary		2,499 96	
S. N. Wood, expenses........	$7J1 67		
J. D. Ellis, expenses.........	875 00		
John L. Williams, expenses ...	810 00		
		2,476 67	
			9,976 59

Normal Schools.

Albany	$85,471 32	
Brockport..............................	4,980 48	
Cortland...............................	10,217 81	
Fredonia...............................	5,079 24	
Potsdam................................	3,804 92	
		109,553 77

Printing.

Legislative	$48,279 21	
Concurrent Resolutions.................	10,401 75	
Binding legislative documents..........	1,212 20	
Notices for publishing Session Laws	465 88	
Official canvass, etc....................	363 02	
Advertising proposals for public printing .	148 60	
Printing notices of Treasurer's balances...	44 25	
Miscellaneous	19,053 18	
		79,968 09

* Transportation.

Comptroller...........................	$70 05	
Treasurer	6 85	
Secretary of State......................	1,040 96	
Secretary of State — boxes	272 25	
Engineer and Surveyor	289 12	
Department of Public Instruction	385 25	
Clerk Court of Appeals.................	174 40	
Attorney-General	57 15	
		2,296 03

* See table on page 53.

* Postage.

Governor	$525	77
Comptroller..........................	805	48
Treasurer	165	41
Secretary of State......................	1,126	44
Engineer and Surveyor	118	77
Attorney-General	349	16
Department of Public Instruction	363	78
Clerk of Court of Appeals..............	320	69
State Board of Health..................	400	00
Commissioners of Charities	300	00
Adjutant-General	385	77
Inspector-General......................	90	00

$4,956 27

Stationery.

For public offices and departments.. ....   5,253 10

Public Buildings.

C. B. Andrews, Superintendent, on account of appropriations for maintenance 124,774 72

Justices of the Supreme Court — First District.

John R. Brady, salary	$6,000	00
C. H. Van Brunt, salary.................	2,000	00
George C. Barrett, salary...............	6,000	00
George P. Andrews, salary	2,000	00
Abrm. R. Lawrence, salary	6,000	00
Noah Davis, salary....................	6,000	00
C. Donohue, salary....................	6,000	00

34,000 00

Second District.

Joseph F. Barnard, salary	$22,200	00
J. O. Dykman, salary	13,450	00
Charles F. Brown, salary...............	9,700	00
C. E. Pratt, salary	7,200	00
E. M. Cullen, salary	7,200	00
W. Bartlett, salary....................	2,400	00
J. W. Gilbert, abridged salary..........	6,000	00

68,150 00

Third District.

A. M. Osborn, salary	$7,200	00
C. R. Ingalls, salary............	7,200	00
T. R. Westbrook, salary	7,200	00
W. L. Learned, salary	7,200	00
R. W. Peckham, salary.................	2,400	00

31,200 00

* See table on page 52.

Fourth District.

C. O. Tappan, salary	$7,200	00
Augustus Bockes, salary	7,200	00
Joseph Potter, salary	7,200	00
J. S. Landon, salary	7,200	00
F. Fish, salary	2,400	00

$31,200 00

Fifth District.

George A. Hardin, salary	$7,200	00
M. H. Marvin, salary	7,200	00
J. C. Churchill, salary	7,200	00
Irving G. Vann, salary	7,200	00
P. C. Williams, salary	2,400	00
George U. Kennedy, salary	2,400	00

33,600 00

Sixth District.

William Murray, salary	$7,200	00
C. E. Martin, salary	7,200	00
D. L. Follett, salary	7,200	00
D. Boardman, salary	7,200	00
H. B. Smith, salary	2,400	00

31,200 00

Seventh District.

F. A. Macomber, salary	$7,200	00
James C. Smith, salary	7,200	00
Charles C. Dwight, salary	7,200	00
George B. Bradley, salary	2,400	00
William Rumsey, salary	7,200	00
J. L. Angle, salary	2,400	00
E. D. Smith, abridged salary	2,183	33

35,783 33

Eighth District.

George Baker, salary	$7,200	00
Charles Daniels, salary	7,200	00
Albert Haight, salary	7,200	00
H. A. Childs, salary	2,400	00
L. C. Lewis, salary	7,200	00
Thomas Corbett, salary	2,400	00
J. L. Talcott, abridged salary	6,000	00

39,600 00

Supreme Court Expenses.

General Term expenses	$3,452	92
Law libraries	11,333	70
Stenographer	5,000	00
Reports sent to other States	344	50

20,131 12

Penitentiaries.

Albany County Penitentiary	$3,954 53	
Erie County Penitentiary	3,190 96	
Kings County Penitentiary	8,196 69	
Monroe County Penitentiary...........	2,208 15	
New York County Penitentiary..........	11,243 66	
Tramps.................................	9,821 96	
		$38,615 95

Refunded Taxes.

For redemption of lands sold for taxes....	$36,451 83	
For erroneous payment of taxes..........	7,748 91	
To county treasurers for non-resident taxes and county treasurers' fees	49,023 50	
		93,224 24

Expenses of Public Lands.

Services and expenses of agents, and serving notices on occupants, etc..........		$6,355 67	
Printing...............................		167 25	
Witnesses, etc		450 00	
Miscellaneous payments		3,650 96	
Clerks, Comptroller's office:			
Frank Brandow	$333 34		
M. G. Graham....	770 00		
F. B. Holdridge..............	750 00		
O. B. V. Taylor	250 00		
W. H. Sanger	1,275 00		
Chas. W. Campbell	100 00		
		3,478 34	
			14,102 22

Indian Affairs.

Annuities..............................	$7,469 43	
Compensation of agents and attorneys, etc.	2,319 68	
		9,789 11

Surveys.

Adirondack survey.....................	$2,500 00	
State survey...........................	13,499 50	
State Land survey.....................	10,000 00	
		25,999 50

State Boundaries.

Expenses of commissioners to settle boundary line of New York and the States of Pennsylvania and New Jersey	2,500 00

Commissioner in Lunacy.

Stephen Smith, Commissioner, salary	$3,999 96	
Stephen Smith, Commissioner, expenses	679 46	
		$4,679 42

Commissioners of Emigration.

Insurance premium Ward's Island property	$64 50	
Philip J. Joachinson, atty., judgment for costs, interest, etc......................	811 32	
		875 82

Agriculture.

Allegany county	$284 82
Broome county	163 31
Cayuga county...........................	368 06
Chautauqua county	348 56
Chemung county..........................	120 34
Cattaraugus county	209 63
Chenango county	297 07
Columbia county..........................	324 19
Cortland county	182 81
Delaware county.........................	258 38
Dutchess county.........................	382 69
Erie county	453 37
Essex county	173 06
Franklin county :........................	121 88
Fulton county...........................	146 25
Genesee county	224 25
Greene county...........................	221 81
Herkimer county.........................	273 00
Hamilton county.........................	41 57
Jefferson county	446 06
Lewis county............................	129 19
Livingston county........................	311 05
Madison county..........................	255 93
Monroe county...........................	472 87
Montgomery county......................	260 81
New York county........................	9,706 25
Niagara county..........................	226 60
Oneida county	621 56
Onondaga county	497 25
Ontario county..........................	316 87
Orange county...........................	370 50
Orleans county...........................	182 81
Oswego county...........................	319 21
Otsego county	360 75
Putnam county..........................	92 63
Queens county...........................	221 81
Rockland county.........................	87 75
Rensselaer county	438 75
St. Lawrence county.....................	414 38

Saratoga county.	$294 94	
Schoharie county	236 44	
Schuyler county.	102 79	
Seneca county.	180 37	
Steuben county	306 54	
Suffolk county.	236 44	
Sullivan county.	114 56	
Tompkins county	235 7J	
Tioga county	148 69	
Warren county.	97 50	
Washington county	299 81	
Wayne county	307 13	
Wyoming county.	237 39	
Yates county	148 69	
American Institute, New York county	2,315 63	
		$25,590 71

Indian Agricultural Societies.

Onondaga Indian Society	$166 66	
(Iroquois) Cattaraugus.	166 66	
Red House Indian Society	166 66	
		499 98

Commissioners of Quarantine.

Salaries	$7,500 00	
Maintenance, etc.	16,079 87	
		23,579 87

Auction Agent.

Alexander Kennedy, agent, salary	$1,200 00	
Alexander Kennedy, agent, expenses	100 00	
		1,300 00

Inspector of Gas Meters.

Ferdinand Ehrhardt, inspector, salary		2,500 00

Washington's Head-quarters.

Maintenance.		1,000 00

Onondaga Salt Springs.

Maintenance.	$61,620 72	
Machinery, etc.	8,000 00	
		69,620 72

Commissioners of Fisheries.

Seth Green, superintendent, maintenance	$15,636 08	
Eugene Blackford, superintendent Cold Spring Hatchery, maintenance, etc.	5,960 49	
		21,596 57

Shore Inspector.

Walter Thorn, Inspector, salary..........	$1,500 00	
Walter Thorn, Inspector, expenses........	875 00	
		$2,375 00

Pilot Commissioners.

Expenses of the board................................ 4,500 00

Public Administrators.

Luke F. Cozzens, services and disbursements as special counsel — Mathias Asholum and R. O'Brien, executors and heirs of W. A. Kennally, deceased, v. State of New York... 4,512 98

Surrogates' Fees.

Surrogate of Allegany county............	$1 60	
Surrogate of Cattaraugus county.........	5 87	
Surrogate of Columbia county...........	1 10	
Surrogate of Delaware county............	75	
Surrogate of Greene county..............	3 00	
Surrogate of New York county..........	28 81	
		41 13

Game and Fish Protectors.

Salaries................................	$6,942 66	
Expenses...............................	2,995 76	
		9,938 42

Hudson River Improvement.

Payments on account of appropriations, etc............ 32,759 59

Roads.

Seth Johnson and Charles N. Holts, commissioners, account resident highway taxes of 1882, Essex county...........	$27 39	
Byron N. Brewster and others, account non-resident highway taxes, Essex county	235 12	
		262 51

Cayuga Inlet.

James Shanahan, Superintendent of Public Works. ... 1,200 00

Commissioners of Niagara Park.

Wm. Dorsheimer, president, etc................... 3,103 44

State Tax.

R. A. Maxwell, Treasurer, Canal Fund, 73-100 mill tax to provide for deficiency in the

5

Canal Sinking Fund, article 7, section 3 of
the Constitution, and chapter 373, Laws of
1883............................$2,054,812 89
Same account, 3-10 mill tax, to provide for
maintenance of the canals, repairs, etc.,
chapter 495, Laws of 1883............   844,443 65
Same for awards made by Canal Appraisers,
being 17-100 mill tax, chapter 471, Laws of
1883................................   47,851 81
                                    ——————————$2,947,108 35

Fugitives from Justice.

N. S. Snyder, services and expenses in arresting James
Cooney, etc...................................   150 00

Rivers, Roads and Bridges.

Constructing bridge across Tonawanda
creek............................. $2,050 00
Eben P. Colton and Luke Usher, com-
missioners, improvement of Racquet river   8,228 45
James Shanahan, Superintendent, account
E. D. Smalley's contract for building
bridge across Tonawanda creek, Tona-
wanda Indian reservation.............   1,950 00
J. M. Harris, commissioner, improvement
Salmon and Mad rivers..............   3,000 00
                                    ——————————   15,228 45

Asylum for Insane Criminals.

Maintenance..................... $29,920 68
Repairs, etc......................   12,898 31
                                    ——————————   42,818 99

Prison Labor Commission.

Salaries............................. $680 00
Expenses...........................   279 63
                                    ——————————   959 63

Forestry Commission.

For expenses...   1,678 70

Tenement-house Commission.

W. P. Easterbrook, treasurer, expenses of Commission
per chapter 448, Laws 1884.....................   300 00

Dairy Commissioner.

J. K. Brown, Commissioner, salary......... $875 00
Postage.............................   148 00
Experts, incidental expenses, etc.........   4,033 68
                                    ——————————   5,056 68

Agricultural Experiment Station.

Maintenance...........................	$19,592 00	
Traveling expenses of members, etc.......	408 00	
		20,000 00

Thomas Asylum.

Maintenance...........................	$10,000 00	
Repairs...............................	1,000 00	
		11,000 00

New York State Institution for Blind, Batavia.

Maintenance and instruction of pupils....	$40,000 00	
Repairs, etc...........................	12,317 16	
		52,317 16

Institution for the Blind, New York city.

For support and instruction of pupils	48,102 79

Institutions for Deaf and Dumb.

Western New York Institution for Deaf-Mutes :.............................	$23,425 34	
Central New York Institution for Deaf-Mutes...............................	28,722 22	
Institution for Improved Instruction of Deaf-Mutes.	21,532 71	
St. Joseph's Institute for Deaf-Mutes.....	29,353 01	
Le Couteulx St. Mary's Institution for Instruction of Deaf and Dumb...........	20,680 35	
Institute for Deaf and Dumb, New York city................................	75,973 48	
		199,687 11

Western House of Refuge.

Maintenance		$58,333 34	
Award of Board of Audit for labor, materials, etc., for construction..................	$10,925 00		
Interest on same	931 49		
		11,856 49	
			70,189 83

State Reformatory, Elmira.

Maintenance	$30,000 00	
Building, etc	14,000 00	
		44,000 00

New York State Soldiers and Sailors' Home.

Maintenance and building......................	90,000 00

Hudson River State Hospital.

Salaries of officers.......................	$9,500 00	
Repairs	4,000 00	
		$13,500 00

State Lunatic Asylum, Utica.

Salaries of officers.......................	$14,927 29	
Repairs	5,000 00	
		19,927 29

Homœopathic Asylum.

Salaries of officers.......................	$8,000 00	
Repairs	5,000 00	
		13,000 00

State Asylum for Insane, Buffalo.

Salaries of officers.......................	$7,535 95	
Building, etc............................	3,848 40	
Construction of sewer.....................	1,957 04	
		13,341 39

Juvenile Delinquents.

Maintenance..............................		70,000 00

Idiot Asylum.

Maintenance.... ....$53,500 00		
Building..................... 10,000 00		
	$63,500 00	
Maintenance of custodial branch.......... 10,000 00		
		73,500 00

Binghamton Asylum for Chronic Insane.

Salaries of officers........	$6,850 00	
Maintenance.............................	2,000 00	
Repairs, etc.............................	29,217 50	
		38,067 50

Willard Asylum for the Insane.

Salaries of officers.......................	$12,500 00	
Maintenance.............................	6,000 00	
Repairs, etc	4,800 00	
		23,300 00

Miscellaneous.

Deaf-mutes' Journal.......................	$650 00
Oswego river dam........................	4,000 00
Bear river dam...........................	80 55
Prosecution of District Attorney, Oneida Co., etc., award of the Board of Audit........	1,321 55

Re-establishing original arms of the State...	$235 00	
Abating nuisances, etc..........................	1,419 97	
Books for town of Clare......................	50 00	
Books for town of Marbletown.............	50 00	
Books for town of St. Armand..............	50 00	
Purchase of land, etc.......................	15,069 99	
James Shanahan, Superintendent, repairs to canal, etc....	262 62	
W. W. Wright, disbursements as Canal Commissioner.............................	120 00	
Award of Board of Audit to employees of Old Capitol and State Hall, chapter 366, Laws of 1884.................................	3,310 76	
Award of Board of Audit for use and occupation of premises adjoining Sing Sing prison.	415 33	
Award of Board of Audit to Thomas R. Griffin, superintendent of canal repairs.......	66 30	
Award of Board of Audit for use of scow...	400 00	
Award of Board of Audit for injury to a horse on Champlain canal..............	77 10	
Bernard Collins, administrator, estate of J. J. Collins, per chap. 317, Laws of 1884...	9,033 39	
Annesley & Vint, picture frames, per chap. 362, Laws of 1882..............	59 75	
Improvement of channel in Shinnecock and Peconic bays..........................	283 65	
		$36,955 96
Tranfers:		
From General Fund to apply on deficiency in Common School Fund..................	$27,056 73	
From General Fund to Elmira Female College Fund for interest..................	301 03	
From General Fund to Literature Fund for interest............................. ...	9 52	
From General Fund to Common School Fund, capital, etc., authorized by chap. 520, Laws of 1883, sale of armory lots in Corning...	2,000 00	
From General Fund to Common School Fund, for interest on money in treasury, per chap. 382, Laws of 1849.....	1,012 46	
From General Fund to United States Deposit Fund, revenue for interest..............	3,520 82	
		33,900 56
Total payments from General Fund $8,259,802 65		

FREE SCHOOL FUND.

Apportionment to Counties.

Albany county............................$75,798 30	
Allegany county........................ 28,043 33	

Broome county	$31,386	11
Cattaraugus county	35,524	49
Cayuga county	37,923	47
Chautauqua county	41,690	09
Chemung county	24,471	01
Chenango county	27,888	52
Clinton county	30,138	08
Columbia county	26,632	07
Cortland county	17,114	94
Delaware county	30,948	54
Dutchess county	42,181	67
Erie county	112,921	98
Essex county	21,725	00
Franklin county	20,916	38
Fulton county	17,715	80
Genesee county	18,489	33
Greene county	19,582	52
Hamilton county	2,943	17
Herkimer county	26,129	96
Jefferson county	43,169	96
Kings county	275,076	79
Lewis county	20,926	31
Livingston county	23,565	90
Madison county	27,588	94
Monroe county	74,834	59
Montgomery county	20,241	49
New York county	574,029	09
Niagara county	30,556	94
Oneida county	68,282	29
Onondaga county	68,978	62
Ontario county	29,006	76
Orange county	48,400	85
Orleans county	17,933	48
Oswego county	46,505	23
Otsego county	33,739	45
Putnam county	8,622	71
Queens county	45,353	73
Rensselaer county	60,344	10
Richmond county	18,262	41
Rockland county	13,893	45
St. Lawrence county	56,474	22
Saratoga county	33,178	60
Schenectady county	13,599	97
Schoharie county	21,404	33
Schuyler county	12,189	74
Seneca county	16,973	51
Steuben county	50,374	98
Suffolk county	28,755	38
Sullivan county	20,061	06
Tioga county	21,305	60
Tompkins county	21,902	73
Ulster county	44,988	86

Warren county..............................	$15,870 35	
Washington county	30,234 60	
Wayne county	30,378 61	
Westchester county	56,312 33	
Wyoming county...........................	19,882 46	
Yates county..............................	12,741 09	
		$2,746,106 77

Normal Schools.

Albany Normal School......................	$17,894 83	
Brockport Normal School..................	18,006 01	
Cortland Normal School..................	18,000 00	
Buffalo Normal School....................	16,086 52	
Fredonia Normal School...................	18,000 00	
Genesee Normal School....................	18,233 12	
Oswego Normal School....................	18,000 00	
Potsdam Normal School...................	17,498 08	
		141,718 56

County Treasurers.

Fees for distributing State school tax......	$13,183 61	
Teachers' institutes	18,303 54	
School commissioners' salaries.............	111,611 12	
		143,098 27

Indian Schools.

Allegany and Cattaraugus Reservation schools	$3,166 38	
Oneida and Madison Reservation schools....	91 61	
Onondaga Reservation schools.............	56 00	
St. Regis Reservation schools..............	187 50	
Shinnecock and Poospatuck Reservation schools	173.95	
Tonawanda Reservation schools.............	317 19	
Tuscarora Reservation schools.............	23 71	
George B. Weaver, traveling expenses visiting Indian schools.........................	9 38	
		4,025 72

Total Free School Fund......................		$3,034,949 32

COMMON SCHOOL FUND.

Apportionment to Counties.

Albany county...	$8,364 72
Allegany county..........................	2,164 31
Broome county...........................	3,251 13
Cattaraugus county.......................	3,572 32
Cayuga county	3,773 82
Chautauqua county	4,050 43
Chemung county	2,755 18
Chenango county	2,132 16
Clinton county....	3,181 21

·Columbia county	$2,938 29
Cortland county.........................	2,118 04
Delaware county.........................	2,357 22
Dutchess county.........................	4,218 95
Erie county.............................	11,030 42
Essex county............................	1,699 21
Franklin county.........................	1,625 58
Fulton county...........................	3,011 44
Genesee county..........................	1,478 00
Greene county...........................	1,541 49
Hamilton county	219 94
Herkimer county	2,855 11
Jefferson county........................	4,149 99
Kings county............................	28,913 36
Lewis county............................	1,613 05
Livingston county	1,864 08
Madison county	2,147 09
Monroe county	6,904 78
Montgomery county......................	1,641 60
Niagara county..........................	2,395 29
New York county........................	51,379 70
Oneida county...........................	5,309 33
Onondaga county........................	5,325 34
Ontario county..........................	2,302 76
Orange county	3,746 85
Orleans county	1,418 77
Oswego county	3,624 81
Otsego county...........................	2,617 23
Putnam county..........................	688 99
Queens county	3,629 38
Rensselaer county.................... ...	4,811 07
Richmond county.........................	1,526 53
Rockland county	1,141 93
St. Lawrence county.....................	4,321 85
Saratoga county	2,569 04
Schenectady county......................	1,032 65
Schoharie county	1,658 37
Schuyler county	946 12
Seneca county...........................	1,300 24
Steuben county..........................	3,810 17
Suffolk county..........................	2,329 80
Sullivan county.........................	1,575 16
Tioga county............................	1,599 79
Tompkins county.. ....,...........	1,656 73
Ulster county...........................	3,651 53
Warren county	1,240 95
Washington county	2,361 76
Wayne county	2,407 01
Westchester county	4,494 67
Wyoming county	1,548 41
Yates county............................	1,004 85

$245,000 00

Indian Schools.

Expenses for maintenance $5,793 81

Transfers .

From capital of Common School Fund to General Fund
for bonds for lands, etc............................ 2,932 75

Total Common School Fund $253,726 56

LITERATURE FUND.

Apportionment.

Addison Union School	$193	89
Adelphi Academy.........................	247	70
Afton Union School......................	73	99
Antrim Academy and High School........	505	05
Albany Academy	241	27
Albany High School......................	2,031	28
Albion Union School.....................	206	36
Alfred University.......................	442	38
Amsterdam Academy......................	48	25
Angola Union School	166	59
Arcade Union School.....................	41	82
Argyle Academy..........................	6	43
Attica Union School	130	72
Aurora Academy..........................	22	52
Avon Union School.......................	91	99
Bainbridge Union School	245	02
Baldwinsville Free Academy	171	28
Batavia Union School.......................	317	96
Binghamton Central High School	411	76
Boonville Union School	58	69
Bridgehampton Lit. and Com'l Institute....	12	87
Brookfield Union School..................	171	20
Brooklyn Coll. and Polytechnic Institute...	672	33
Buffalo Central School...................	1,235	10
Cambridge Union School..................	24	08
Camden Union School....................	25	74
Canandaigua Academy	142	86
Canaseraga Union School.................	38	60
Canastota Union School	61	90
Candor Free Academy.....................	79	34
Canisteo Academy	154	94
Canton Union School	77	20
Carthage Union School...................	57	90
Cary Collegiate Seminary	38	60
Castile Union School.....................	95	64
Catskill Free Academy....................	101	86
Cazenovia Seminary......................	371	51
Chamberlain Institute....................	167	28

Chester Union School	$16 08
Canajoharie Union School	83 12
Chateaugay Union School	61 12
Cincinnatus Academy	86 34
Claverack Academy and H. R. Institute	313 05
Clinton Grammar School	33 74
Clinton Liberal Institute..................	183 36
Clyde High School......................	64 34
Cobleskill Union School..................	137 37
Colgate Academy	35 39
Cook Academy	152 98
Cooperstown Union School.................	288 23
Corning Free Academy...................	207 06
Coxsackie Union School...................	48 25
Crown Point Union School................	9 65
Cuba Union School	53 25
Delaware Academy......................	146 94
Delaware Literary Institute	116 29
Deposit Union School....................	41 82
DeRuyter Union School	25 74
Dryden Union School	83 47
Dunkirk Union School...................	221 45
Dundee Preparatory School	112 50
Egberts High School...................	150 94
Ellington Union School	25 74
Elizabethtown Union School..............	130 47
Elmira Free Academy....................	398 90
East Springfield Academy	9 65
Fayetteville Union Seminary..............	61 12
Falley Seminary	12 87
Fairfield Academy	73 47
Fairport Union School....................	49 04
Flushing High School....................	93 29
Forestville Free Academy..........	175 19
Fort Covington Free Academy	83 12
Fort Edward Collegiate Institute	138 32
Fort Edward Union School	3 22
Franklin Free Academy	373 35
Franklin Academy and Union School	136 72
Friendship Academy	45 04
Fulton Union School.....................	145 89
Genesee Valley Sem. and Union School.....	25 74
Genesee Wesleyan Seminary..............	218 75
Geneva Classical and Union School	264 10
Gilbertsville Academy....................	103 90
Glens Falls Academy....................	359 61
Gloversville Union School	186 58
Gouverneur Wesleyan Seminary	317 53
Gowanda Union School..	71 55
Greene Union School.....................	67 39
Greeneville Academy....................	54 69
Greenwich Union School.................	125 20

Griffith Institute	$115 81
Groton Union School	122 24
Hamburgh Union School	73 99
Hancock Union School	25 74
Hartwick Seminary	104 99
Haverling Union School	492 46
Holland Patent Union School	32 17
Holly Union School	22 52
Homer Union School	290 15
Hoosick Falls Union School	73 99
Horseheads Union School	28 95
Houghton Seminary	61 12
Howell Free Academy	239 36
Hudson Academy	12 87
Huntington Union School	181 71
Ilion Union School	376 93
Ingham University	56 25
Ithaca High School	715 44
Ives Seminary	147 98
Jamestown Union School	611 23
Johnstown Union School	359 92
Jordan Free Academy	175 19
Keeseville Union School	16 08
Kingston Academy	370 25
Kinderhook Academy	22 52
Lansingburgh Academy	88 77
Lawrenceville Academy	113 37
Leavenworth Free Institute and Union School	48 25
Leonardsville Union School	9 65
Le Roy Academic Institute	159 20
Liberty Normal Institute	39 39
Limestone Union School	48 25
Lisle Union School	51 47
Little Falls Union School	157 63
Liverpool Union School	32 17
Lockport Union School	604 70
Lowville Academy	83 64
Lyons Union School	336 58
Macedon Academy	92 99
Madison Union School	44 17
McGrawville Union School	28 95
Manlius Union School	41 82
Massena Union School	48 25
Moriah Union School	315 00
Marathon Union School	35 39
Marion Collegiate Institute	126 24
Mayville Union School	112 59
Mechanicsville Academy	54 69
Medina Free Academy	119 81
Mexico Academy	126 24
Moravia Union School	156 68
Morris Union School	72 60

Mt. Morris Union School...................	$67 55
Munro Collegiate Institute	243 36
Newark Union School	180 24
New Berlin Union School.................	135 86
Naples Union School	64 34
Nunda Union School.....................	99 72
New Lots Union School..................	102 34
New Paltz Academy......................	41 82
New Rochelle Union School..............	67 55
Nichols Union School	9 65
North Tarrytown Union School...........	16 08
Ogdensburg Free Academy...............	257 35
Olean Union School.....................	115 81
Oneonta Union School...................	208 81
Onondaga Free Academy.........	133 68
Oswego High School....................	402 38
Owego Free Academy....................	950 01
Oxford Academy........................	144 81
Ovid Union School.....................	32 17
Packer Collegiate Institute...............	501 83
Painted Post Union School..............	54 69
Palatine Bridge Union School...........	9 65
Palmyra Classical Union School...........	370 40
Parker Union School....................	145 20
Penn Yan Academy..........	159 19
Perry Union School	194 76
Phelps Union and Classical School........	141 94
Phœnix Union School	223 10
Pike Seminary..........................	110 16
Plattsburgh High School.................	185 81
Pompey Academy.......................	58 69
Port Byron Free School and Academy......	152 24
Port Henry Union School................	58 69
Port Jervis Union School	500 00
Portville Union School	25 74
Poughkeepsie High School...............	248 66
Pulaski Academy	185 98
Putnam Union School...................	13 65
Red Creek Union Seminary	109 29
Rensselaerville Academy.................	74 17
Rochester Female Academy...............	12 87
Rochester Free Academy.................	926 46
Rome Free Academy	336 04
Rushville Union School..................	41 82
Rushford Union School..................	3 22
Sandy Creek Union School..............	232 68
Sandy Hill Union School.................	257 02
Sherman Union School	86 69
Saratoga Springs Union School	164 06
Schenectady Union Classical Institute......	398 90
Schoharie Union School	186 89
Sauquoit Academy......................	57 90

Sinclairville Union School	$73 12
Schuylerville Union School	52 60
Schenevus Union School	112 77
Seymour Smith Academy	120 34
Seneca Falls (Free) Academy	268 15
Sherburne Union School	150 16
Silver Creek Union School	121 34
Skaneateles Union School	183 32
Smithville Union School	52 25
Sodus Academy	221 58
Spencer Union School	53 04
Starkey Seminary	125 46
Syracuse High School	1,225 63
Sherman Academy	112 59
Ten Broeck Free Academy	97 29
Troy Academy	32 17
Troy High School	514 70
Trumansburgh Union School	70 77
Unadilla Academy	73 12
Union Academy of Belleville	48 25
Utica (Free) Academy	558 24
Vernon Union School	9 56
Walton Union School	123 50
Walrath Academy	199 45
Wallkill Free Academy	125 46
Warrensburgh Academy	3 22
Warsaw Union School	109 99
Washington (Free) Academy	109 77
Waterford Union School	19 30
Warwick Institute	71 63
Westerlo Union School	151 81
Watertown High School	295 95
Waterville Union School	180 59
Watkins Academic Union School	73 99
Waverly Union School	172 84
Weedsport Union School	115 29
Westchester Union School	23 30
Westfield Union School	265 54
West Hebron Union School	35 39
Westport Union School	9 65
West Winfield Academy	66 12
Whitehall Union School	77 99
Whitney's Point Union School	59 47
Wilson Union School	93 29
Woodhull Union School	12 87
Yates Academy	6 43
Yates Union School	291 71

$39,958 18

Purchase of Books and Apparatus.

Albany Academy	$137 00
Adams Collegiate Institute	150 00

Addison Union School	$131 99
Afton Union School	15 00
Avon Union School	150 00
Baldwinsville Union School	128 67
Bainbridge Union School	130 18
Clyde High School	150 00
Cazenovia Seminary	150 00
Canastota Union School	121 56
Canton Union School	150 00
Chester Union School	50 00
Clinton Grammar School	150 00
Dryden Union School	16 67
Delaware Literary Institute	100 00
Dundee Preparatory School	50 00
Delaware Academy	41 53
Fort Covington Free Academy	86 87
Flushing High School	102 50
Groton Union School	150 00
Greenwich Union School	100 00
Griffith Institute and Union School	103 31
Glens Falls Academy	50 00
Gowanda Union School	122 92
Holland Patent Union School	150 00
Houghton Academy	100 00
Hamburgh Union School	85 00
Ithaca High School	50 00
Ilion Union School	138 35
Johnstown Union School	148 79
Lansingburgh Academy	56 00
Le Roy Academic Institute	124 28
Lockport Union School	150 00
Limestone Union School	120 19
Madison Union School	60 50
Moravia Union School	131 54
Mt. Morris Union School	48 22
Massena Union School	48 00
New Paltz Academy	150 00
Olean Union School	150 00
Ogdensburg Free Academy	80 00
Oswego High School	144 15
Oxford Academy	35 00
Phœnix Union School	143 80
Port Byron Union School and Academy	50 00
Palatine Bridge Union School	50 00
Penn Yan Academy	150 00
Pulaski Academy	150 00
Sherburne Union School	42 00
Seymour Smith Academy	40 00
Silver Creek Union School	142 00
Spencer Union School	90 45
Unadilla Academy	50 00
Westfield Union School	150 00

Warsaw Union School.....................	$73 92	
Washington Free Academy.................	123 37	
Watkins Academic Union School..........	40 00	
Yates Academy..........................	137 91	
		$5,941 67
Total Literature Fund..........		$45,899 85

UNITED STATES DEPOSIT FUND.

Instruction of Common School Teachers.

Albany High School......................	$500 00
Addison Union School....................	69 00
Afton Union School......................	110 00
Angola Union School.....................	351 00
Albion Academy.........................	426 00
Adams Collegiate Institute...............	247 00
Ausable Forks Union School..............	44 00
Alfred University.......................	264 00
Arcade Union School.....................	59 00
Bainbridge Union School.................	125 00
Boonville Union School..................	90 00
Baldwinsville Free Academy..............	233 00
Canton Union School....................	139 00
Canisteo Academy.......................	414 00
Candor Free Academy....................	130 00
Castile Union School....................	137 00
Chamberlain Institute...................	150 00
Cincinnatus Academy....................	314 00
Claverack Academy and H. R. Institute....	223 00
Cobleskill Union School.................	114 00
Canaseraga Union School.................	105 00
Canandaigua Academy....................	40 00
Clyde High School......................	78 00
Crown Point Union School...............	50 00
Delaware Academy.......................	203 00
Forrestville Free Academy...............	151 00
Fairfield Seminary......................	164 00
Fort Edward Collegiate Institute...........	132 25
Franklin Academy and Union School.......	393 00
Fulton Union School....................	174 00
Fort Covington Free Academy.............	350 00
Glens Falls Academy	232 00
Gowanda Union School.	77 00
Gouverneur Union School	143 00
Greenville Academy.....................	130 00
Griffith Institute.......................	222 00
Groton Union School....................	131 00
Hamburgh Union School	36 00
Haverling Union School..................	200 00
Holland Patent Union School......... ...	102 00

Homer Union School......................	$135 00	
Ives Seminary	250 00	
Jamestown Union School and Collegiate Institute	250 00	
Lansingburgh Academy....................	208 00	
Lawrenceville Academy...................	230 00	
Lisle Union School.......................	252 00	
Massena Union School....................	93 00	
Macedon Academy........................	156 00	
Mexico Academy..........	282 00	
Munro Collegiate Institute................	397 00	
Moriah Union School.................	202 00	
Morris Union School	70 00	
Naples Union School.....................	176 00	
Nunda Academy...........................	104 00	
Oswego Free Academy.....................	214 00	
Ogdensburg Academy.....................	326 00	
Oxford Academy.	113 00	
Onondaga Academy.......................	246 00	
Perry Union School......................	143 00	
Pompeer Academy........................	23 00	
Phœnix Union School..............	250 00	
Penn Yan Academy.......................	164 00	
Pulaski Academy	420 00	
Pike Seminary............................	456 00	
Port Byron Free School and Academy......	250 00	
Pompey Academy.........................	78 00	
Rushville Union School...................	142 00	
Sandy Creek Union School................	111 00	
Sanquoit Academy.............	57 00	
Schoharie Union School	65 00	
Sherburne Union School..................	83 00	
Sherman Academy........................	310 00	
Sodus Academy...........................	500 00	
Unadilla Academy........................	130 00	
Union Academy of Belleville	72 00	
Walworth Academy	340 00	
Warsaw Union School.....................	102 00	
Waverly High School......................	70 00	
Westfield Union School.......	228 00	
Weedsport Union School..................	194 00	
Whitney's Point Union School.............	99 00	
Wilson Union School......................	81 00	
Woodhull Union School...................	60 00	
Yates Union School......................	444 00	
		$15,950 35
Inspection of teachers' classes	$2,918 11	
Examination of teachers..................	8,197 47	
New York city armory bonds..............	200,000 00	
		211,115 58

Transfers :

To capital of Common School Fund........	$25,000	00
To revenue of Common School Fund for dividends to common schools...............	75,000	00
To revenue of Literature Fund for dividends to academies..........................	28,000	00
From the revenue to the capital of the U. S. Deposit Fund per chap. 150, Laws 1837, for premises bid in for the State in 1883.....	4,500	00
For failure of title......................	300	00
For loss on sales.......................	950	50

$133,750 50

Total U. S. Deposit Fund....................... $360,816 43

Elmira Female College Educational Fund.

Paid college in full..............................	$20,073	53

Total Elmira Female College Educational Fund... $20,073 53

Military Record Fund.

Bureau of Military Statistics......................	$1,288	08

Total Military Record Fund..................... $1,288 08

Bounty Debt Sinking Fund.

Reimbursement of State stock, seven per cent bounty loan of 1877, principal...........	$3,000	00
Interest from January 1 to April 7, 1877, and $18.60 premium	55	80

$3,055 80

Total Bounty Debt Sinking Fund............... $3,055 80

Canal Fund.

Superintendent of Public Works	$330,431	41
Superintendent of Public Works, salary and travel	6,159	52
Superintendent of Public Works, office expenses	11,606	32
Superintendent of Public Works, collectors and inspectors........................	24,472	87
Assistant Superintendent of Public Works, salary and travel.....................	11,191	43
State Engineer and Surveyor............	200	00

7

Division engineers	$28,129	33
Superintendents of repairs.............	385,165	64
Superintendents of repairs, salaries......	22,719	72
Clerk's bureau canal affairs.............	5,286	88
Allowance by Canal Board...............	100	00
Advertising	6	87
Tolls refunded.........................	7	68
Legal services	4,585	09
Interest on awards	1,082	77
Salary Canal Commissioner	433	33
Fort Miller Bridge Company.............	1,000	00
Examining abstracts of title	12	50
Washing towels........................	12	00
Express charges	6	75
Telegraphing..........................		67
Stationery	59	38
Keeping transfer office	1,250	00
Salary transfer agent...................	750	00
Interest on stocks.....................	500,310	00
Redemption of stocks	9,000	00
Purchase of bonds as investments for Sinking Fund	1,640,000	00

$2,983,980 16

Total Canal Fund $2,983,980 16

RECAPITULATION.

General Fund	$8,259,802	65
Common School Fund..............................	253,726	56
Free School Fund..................................	3,034,949	32
Literature Fund..................................	45,899	85
United States Deposit Fund	360,816	43
College Land Scrip Fund...........................	....	
Elmira Female College Educational Fund	20,073	53
Military Record Fund..............................	1,288	08
Canal Fund....	2,983,980	16
Bounty Debt Sinking Fund.........................	3,055	80

Total payments.............................$14,963,592 38

STATEMENT showing the condition of the treasury, October 1, 1884.

FUNDS.	Balances in treasury, Oct. 1, 1883.	Receipts for fiscal year ending Sept. 30, 1884.	Payments for fiscal year ending Sept. 30, 1884.	Balance in treasury, Oct. 1, 1884.	Deficiencies in funds, Oct. 1, 1884.	Deficiencies in funds, Oct. 1, 1883.	Total cash balance in treasury, Oct. 1, 1884.
General	$1,132,728 80	$8,636,683 11	$8,259,802 65	$1,709,607 26			
Common School	......	815,464 92	258,728 56	......	$7,064 65	$65,808 01	
Free School	285,419 15	3,104,313 18	3,034,949 32	304,783 01			
Literature	2,929 88	42,139 08	45,899 85	......	831 47		
United States Deposit	56,845 92	345,047 79	360,816 43	41,077 28			
College Land Scrip	85,898 69	19,287 71	20,073 53	55,074 80			
Elmira Female College Educational	12,315 00	7,758 53	1,288 08	......			
Military Record	4,756 20	2,830 27	......	6,296 39			
Canal	972,172 68	8,070,689 12	2,963,980 16	1,058,881 59			
Bounty Debt Sinking	3,055 80	......	3,065 80	......			
	$2,456,067 45	$15,744,163 65	$14,963,562 38	$3,175,721 83	$7,896 12	$65,808 01	$3,167,825 71

STATEMENT showing Monthly Payments for Postage for the Fiscal Year ending September 30, 1884.

OFFICE OR DEPARTMENT.	1883.			1884.									Total.
	October.	November.	December.	January.	February.	March.	April.	May.	June.	July.	August.	September.	
Governor	$55 37	$100 00	$100 00	$108 69	$100 00	$50 00	$55 55	$100 00	$50 00	$6 16	$50 00	$50 00	$525 77
Secretary of State	206 22	100 00		106 33		100 00	5 65		100 00	106 24	100 00	100 00	1,126 44
Comptroller	104 98		60 00	107 30		140 08	21 88	100 00	11 47	118 87	18 44	22 51	805 43
Treasurer	53 38		15 00	5 37	50 00		8 86		50 00	3 22			165 41
State Engineer and Surveyor	88 45	30 00		83 76			83 94				3 32		118 77
Attorney-General	34 60		50 00	84 56			100 00				100 00	50 00	349 16
Department of Public Instruction	53 81			6 52	50 00	50 00	3 83	50 00		54 62			368 78
Clerk of the Court of Appeals	103 90			7 15	100 00		4 66	100 00	100 00	4 98			320 69
State Board of Health	100 00	50 00		50 00				50 00	50 00		100 00		320 00
Commissioners of Public Charities	40 00				35 00			25 00				40 00	400 00
Adjutant-General	198 37			4 88	175 00	30 00	5 52			30 00			300 00
Inspector-General	10 00			10 00		10 00		10 00	10 00	4 02	10 00	30 00	90 00
Total	$942 06	$280 00	$225 00	$523 54	$510 00	$380 08	$358 64	$435 00	$371 47	$328 21	$381 76	$292 51	$4,066 27

STATEMENT showing Monthly Payments for the Transportation of Packages for the fiscal year ending September 30, 1884.

OFFICE OR DEPARTMENT.	1883.			1884.									Total.
	October.	November.	December.	January.	February.	March.	April.	May.	June.	July.	August.	September.	
Secretary of State	$220 90	$390 10	$297 65	$390 05	$11 00	$35 40	$42 70	$4 15	$25 72	$14 65	$226 92	$34 57	$1,818 21
Comptroller	20 65	7 40	2 95	6 20	2 20	2 85	4 10	5 60	6 80	4 30	4 05	2 95	70 06
Treasurer	25	8 65	1 20		12 55					55	1 20		6 85
State Engineer and Surveyor	9 40	133 15	46 92	29 20		10 55	14 70	8 30	7 30	4 75	5 60	6 70	299 12
Attorney-General			29 90	11 70			5 60	2 85			5 45	15 55	57 15
Departm't of Public Instruct'n	137 96	1 25	3 70	2 60	7 05	10 50	8 75	9 40	88 65	123 60	15 25	8 10	385 25
Clerk of the Court of Appeals	23 00	13 70	16 50	15 50		13 35			23 80	28 95		1 15	174 40
Total	$412 15	$549 25	$388 82	$145 25	$32 80	$72 65	$75 85	$30 30	$147 27	$174 20	$258 47	$69 02	$2,296 08

RECEIPTS FROM CORPORATIONS FOR TAXES FROM OCTOBER 1, 1883, TO OCTOBER 1, 1884.

CLASS I. INSURANCE COMPANIES.

Albany..	$1,412 61
Agricultural, Watertown........................	2,830 66
American Fire, New York........................	2,113 89
American Exchange Fire.........................	699 79
American, Boston...............................	215 41
American, Newark, N. J.........................	293 92
American Central, St. Louis....................	334 75
Atlantic Fire & Marine	91 27
Atlantic Mutual................................	26,633 32
Ætna, Hartford................................	3,859 82
American Fire, Philadelphia....................	809 52
Buffalo German................................	1,663 31
Broadway, New York............................	975 25
Buffalo.......................................	542 68
Brooklyn Fire	1,079 19
Boylston Mutual...............................	391 23
Boatman's Fire & Marine, Pittsburgh............	276 10
Boston Marine	3,074 83
British American, Toronto, Canada	476 90
British & Foreign Marine	1,024 50
Commerce, Albany..............................	885 77
City Fire, New York	814 70
Citizens', New York...........................	2,368 33
Commercial Fire, New York	1,185 13
Continental, New York.........................	5,713 53
Clinton Fire, New York........................	1,199 27
Citizens', Pittsburgh.........................	343 62
Commercial Mutual, New York...................	1,377 07
Concordia Fire................................	110 72
California, San Francisco.....................	138 69
China Mutual, Boston..........................	396 83
Commercial Union, New York	3,239 43
Connecticut Fire..............................	1,102 91
Detroit Fire & Marine.........................	87 70
Dutchess County Mutual Fire	586 75
Empire City Fire, New York....................	548 87
Exchange Fire, New York.......................	753 62
Erie County Mutual, Buffalo	279 08
Equitable Fire & Marine, Providence, R. I.....	263 60
Eliot, Boston.................................	115 20
Eagle Fire, New York..........................	1,896 02
Farragut Fire, New York.......................	1,145 50
Franklin & Emporium, New York.................	1,205 78
Firemen's, New York...........................	630 49
Firemen's Trust, Brooklyn.....................	613 41

Fire Insurance Company of the County of Philadelphia.	$239 16
Farmers' Fire, York, Pa...............................	247 57
Fidelity & Casualty.................................	1,692 46
Firemen's, Dayton, Ohio.............................	223 52
Fire Association of Philadelphia.....................	1,794 96
Franklin Fire, Philadelphia.........................	702 10
Firemen's Fund, California..........................	547 52
First National Fire, Worcester, Mass................	62 25
Firemen's, Newark..................................	317 31
Fire Insurance Association (limited), London	933 20
Firemen's, Baltimore...............................	76 22
Guardian Fire, New York............................	400 60
Germania, New York................................	5,096 00
Globe Fire, New York..............................	1,108 50
Glens Falls, New York..	1,858 79
German American..................................	7,410 23
Girard Fire & Marine, Philadelphia..................	110 75
Guardian' Assurance, London........................	1,714 40
German Fire.......................................	302 75
General, Dresden..................................	635 55
Great Western Marine..............................	2,989 74
Germania, Newark, N. J............................	194 00
Greenwich...	5,177 63
Howard Fire, New York.............................	1,532 24
Home, New York...................................	12,175 06
Hanover Fire, New York	4,614 12
Hamburg Bremen Fire	1,216 83
Hartford Fire	2,412 05
Hartford Steam Boiler Inspection and Insurance.......	399 19
Hamilton Fire, New York...........................	936 26
Irving, New York..................................	300 00
Importers & Traders', New York.....................	300 00
Insurance Company of the State of Pennsylvania.......	458 29
Insurance Company of North America	4,994 39
Imperial, London..................................	1,606 80
Jefferson, New York	1,140 96
Knickerbocker, New York...........................	784 62
Kings County Fire.................................	1,246 94
La Fayette Fire, Brooklyn	854 45
Lorillard, New York...............................	324 00
Long Island.......................................	1,702 07
Lloyds Plate Glass, New York	150 00
Liverpool & London Globe..........................	6,426 35
Lancashire, Manchester............................	1,755 92
London Assurance Corporation......................	1,209 92
London Provincial Fire, New York agency............	890 36
London & Lancashire Fire, Liverpool	2,380 05
Mercantile, Cleveland..............................	139 32
Merchants', Providence, R. I.......................	300 94
Metropolitan Plate Glass...........................	659 46
Manufacturers & Builders' Fire	1,080 08
Mercantile Fire, New York	408 07

Mechanics' Fire, Brooklyn	$1,231 11
Mutual, Albany	83 92
Mercantile Fire & Marine, Boston	114 20
Michigan Fire & Marine, Detroit	170 82
Mechanics,' Philadelphia	323 60
Montauk Fire	931 25
Mutual Benefit Policy, Loan & Trust	87 00
Merchants,' New Jersey	746 64
Merchants,' New York	983 50
Merchants & Traders' Fire, New York	1,048 43
New York Equitable	859 88
New York Life	6,250 00
New York Fire	1,021 72
North River, New York	853 40
Nassau Fire	888 80
New York Bowery Fire	2,070 19
National Fire, New York	1,286 64
Niagara Fire	3,139 33
Northwestern National, Milwaukee	154 81
Neptune Fire & Marine, Boston	104 03
North American	128 40
Newark Fire	277 07
Norwich Union Fire	1,313 19
North German Fire, Hamburg, Germany	326 93
National Fire, Hartford	349 18
New Hampshire Fire, Manchester	277 52
New York Mutual	1,413 52
Northern Assurance	1,147 78
New Orleans	486 35
Orient, Hartford	555 96
Orient Mutual, New York	1,547 46
Pacific Fire, New York	1,537 38
Park Fire	924 22
Peter Cooper Fire	646 34
People's Fire, New York	1,026 84
Pennsylvania Fire	861 18
Providence Washington, Providence, R. I	2,256 05
Pennsylvania, Pittsburgh	313 51
Prescott, Boston	343 66
Phœnix, Hartford	1,983 08
Phœnix, New York	7,837 80
Phœnix Assurance, London	1,667 63
Queen	1,339 47
Rutgers Fire, New York	788 30
Rochester German	1,245 31
Royal, Liverpool	3,591 46
Sea, New York	3,381 73
Sun Mutual	735 49
Standard Fire, New York	719 28
Star Fire, New York	1,435 52
Sterling Fire	765 96
Stuyvesant, New York	1,196 27

Security, New Haven	$309 94
Spring Garden, Philadelphia	177 78
Suffolk Mutual......................................	46 32
Standard Fire office, London...............	688 57
St. Paul's Fire & Marine	275 49
Switzerland Marine, Zurich...........................	1,936 82
Springfield Fire & Marine, Springfield	988 41
Sun, San Francisco..................................	113 40
Shoe & Leather, Boston	465 17
Tradesmen's Fire, New York	1,125 00
Thames & Mersey Marine............................	974 48
Transatlantic Fire, Hamburgh	379 38
Traders', Chicago...................................	646 96
United States Fire, New York........................	993 52
Union Fire, Buffalo.................................	321 19
Union Marine, Liverpool.............................	1,365 16
Union, Philadelphia.................................	247 52
United States Branch of the North British & Mercantile ..	2,434 76
Union of California.................................	121 16
United Firemen's, Philadelphia......................	228 48
Universal Marine, London............................	172 16
Venice Town, Genoa.................................	30
Westchester Fire, New York.........................	2,114 29
Williamsburgh City Fire.............................	3,636 95
Washington Fire & Marine...........................	705 06
Western Assurance, Toronto, Canada.................	740 80
	$248,013 15

CLASS II.   TRANSPORTATION.

Allegany Central R. R. Co...........................	$416 25
Adirondack R. R. Co................................	929 27
Avon, Geneseo & Mt. Morris R. R. Co...............	202 50
Albany & Vermont R. R. Co.........................	450 00
Amsterdam Street R. R. Co..........................	37 76
Adirondack, N. Y. & N. E. Express..................	69 71
Albany Railway.....................................	948 27
Albany & Troy Steamboat...........................	80 92
Atlantic Avenue R. R. — Brooklyn...................	3,493 41
American Refrigerator & Transportation.............	11 97
Addison & Northern Pennsylvania R. R..............	149 50
Adams Express......................................	71 14
Astoria Ferry.......................................	262 72
American Express...................................	6,704 48
Bradford, Eldred & Cuba R. R......................	335 65
Buffalo & South-western R. R.......................	1,908 42
Buffalo, New York & Philadelphia R. R..............	10,398 98
Buffalo, Pittsburgh & Western R. R.................	1,033 96
Broadway & Bowery Bay R. R.......................	2 25
Brooklyn City R. R.................................	17,701 77

8

Brighton R. R.	$15 00
Buffalo Creek R. R.	1,064 87
Buffalo Creek Transfer R. R.	7 50
Binghamton & Port Dickinson R. R.	86 76
Broadway R. R. — Brooklyn	2,976 13
Boston & Albany R. R.	12,005 20
Broadway & Seventh Avenue R. R.	8,994 03
Brooklyn City & Newtown R. R.	2,915 34
Bleecker St. & Fulton Ferry R. R.	283 50
Brighton Pier & Nav. — Brooklyn	187 50
Bushwick R. R.	2,863 35
Buffalo & Grand Island Ferry	20 73
Buffalo Erie Basin R. R.	20 25
Brooklyn Crosstown R. R.	1,691 10
Buffalo, N. Y. & Erie R. R.	1,662 50
Brooklyn & Rockaway Beach R. R.	161 65
Buffalo East Side St. Ry.	578 32
Buffalo St. Railway	1,574 03
Boston, Hoosac Tunnel & Westport R. R.	1,659 85
Brooklyn, Flatbush & Coney Island R. R.	711 03
Bath & Hammondsport R. R.	77 02
Conesus Lake R. R.	7 92
Catskill & Hudson Steam Ferry	58 29
Catskill & Albany Steamboat	213 11
Coney Island & Rockaway R. R.	22 50
Chateaugay R. R.	112 50
Crooked Lake Nav. — Penn Yan	56 08
Canandaigua Lake Steam Nav.	101 27
Central City R. R. — Syracuse	206 21
Cortland & Homer Horse R. R.	41 22
Cooperstown & Susquehanna Valley R. R.	256 63
Clove Branch R. R.	107 89
Central Crosstown R. R. — New York	1,693 00
Chemung R. R. — Baltimore	570 00
Central Park, N. & E. River R. R.	7,506 21
Christopher & Tenth St. R. R.	2,088 77
Coney Island & Brooklyn R. R.	1,868 01
Cornell Steamboat — Rondout	3,217 52
Cayuga & Susquehanna R. R.	1,325 50
Commercial Navigation	28 50
Corning, Cowanesque & Antrim R. R.	3,321 03
Central Tunnel Railway — New York	15 00
Connecting Terminal R. R. — Philadelphia	30 00
Citizens' Steamboat	1,685 30
Cheeney's Towing Line	500 00
Canal & Lake Steamboat — Philadelphia	597 72
Coney Island Elevated R. R.	63 26
Catskill Ferry	42 23
City R. R. — Poughkeepsie	93 08
Conesus Lake Transportation	8 84
Delaware & Hudson Canal	58,937 80
Dry Dock, East Broadway & Battery R. R.	9,426 89

Dunkirk, Allegheny Valley & Pittsburgh R. R	$648 48
Dunkirk & Fredonia R. R...........................	124 39
Delaware, Lackawanna & Western Express............	327 40
Delaware, Lackawanna & Western R. R..............	24,311 64
De Bary Baya Merchants' Line	143 63
Elmira & Horseheads R. R..........................	97 62
East River Ferry..................................	1,944 42
Eighth Avenue R. R	8,140 78
Elmira State Line R. R............................	51 10
Elmira, Jefferson & Canandaigua R. R	750 00
Eastern Transportation Line	778 79
Elmira & Williamsport R. R	129 14
East Genesee Street & Seward Avenue R. R	82 55
Forty-second Street & Grand Street Ferry R. R.......:.	4,552 22
Fifth Ward R. R. — Syracuse	132 18
Frankfort & Ilion Street R. R	43 32
Fonda, Johnstown & Gloversville R. R	1,500 57
Fruit Merchants' Steamship Association	30 00
Fonda & Fultonville Horse R. R.....................	8 81
Genesee Valley Canal..............................	39 06
Greenwich & Johnsville R. R.......................	369 98
Goshen & Deckertown R. R.........................	57 71
Glens Falls Transportation.........................	126 42
Genesee & Water Street R. R.......................	36 00
Greene R. R.......................................	300 00
Grand Street & Newtown Street R. R	916 23
Geneva & Lyons R. R	22
Geneva, Ithaca & Sayre R. R......................	2,384 70
Greenpoint Ferry	1,465 18
Greenport & Shelter Island Ferry..................	58 46
Grand Street, Prospect Park & Flatbush R. R.........	839 14
Garrison & West Point Ferry......................	41 87
Harlem Bridge, Morrisania & Fordham R. R..........	1,150 49
Hartford & Connecticut Western R. R...............	1,201 73
Herkimer & Mohawk Street R. R....................	51 30
Hudson River Line.................................	1,073 00
Houston, West Street & Pavonia Ferry R. R	1,397 89
Herkimer, Newport & Poland R. R..................	331 71
Harlem River & Port Chester R. R..................	63 24
Harlem & New York Navigation.....................	50 62
Homer Ramsdell Transportation.....................	553 75
Iron Steamboat — New York........................	450 00
Johnstown, Gloversville & Kingsboro................	82 50
Jerome Park R. R..................................	43 29
Kingston City R. R	237 14
Keuka Navigation — Penn Yan..	31 60
Knickerbocker Steamboat...........................	583 58
Kaaterskill R. R. — Rondout.......................	93 48
Lackawanna & Pittsburgh R. R.....................	36 97
Lehigh Valley R. R	603 60
Lehigh Valley Transportation	525 00
Lake Shore & Michigan Southern R. R..............	10,180 69

Lansingburgh & Cohoes R. R.	$31 50
Lehigh & Hudson River R. R.	463 05
Long Island R. R.	23,387 06
Lake Champlain & Moriah R. R.	1,418 19
Lake George Steamboat	959 12
Montgomery & Erie R. R.	243 75
Mohawk & Ilion Horse R. R.	58 28
Manhattan Railway	38,705 35
Metropolitan Railway	8,190 00
Middletown & Crawford R. R.	183 30
Middletown, Unionville & Water Gap R. R.	402 51
Montauk R. R.	1,477 50
Marine R. R.	75 00
Manhattan Transfer	102 17
Middleburgh & Schoharie R. R.	45 39
New York & Manhattan Beach R. R.	1,036 49
New York, West Shore & Buffalo R. R.	15,008 42
New York, Pennsylvania & Ohio R. R.	160 75
New York, Catskill & Athens Steamboat	767 98
New York & Staten Island Steamboat	1,100 50
New York, Chicago & St. Louis R. R.	3,676 82
New York, Lake Champlain Transportation	1,394 96
Ninth Avenue R. R.	1,121 83
Niagara Falls Branch R. R.	375 00
Nyack & Northern R. R.	1 13
Northern R. R. of New Jersey	141 18
New York Elevated R. R.	12,761 64
New York, New Haven & Hartford R. R.	10,948 26
New York, Lake Erie & Western R. R.	120,588 11
New York, Lackawanna & Western R. R.	12,450 00
New York & Coney Island R. R.	250 00
New York & Saugerties Transportation	56 53
New York & Philadelphia Coal & Stone Transportation.	61 20
New Jersey Steamboat	4,809 47
New York & Sea Beach R. R.	590 36
New York & New England R. R.	3,426 82
North Second Street & Middle Village R. R.	9 75
Niagara Falls, Suspension Bridge Ry.	112 46
New Williamsburgh & Flatbush R. R.	960 42
New York Transfer	1,110 00
New York & Harlem R. R.	27,597 09
New York Central & Hudson River R. R.	302,485 39
Niagara Bridge & Canandaigua R. R.	1,500 00
Northern Boatmen's Transportation	1 50
New York & Hudson Steamboat	135 58
New York & Boston Dispatch Express	9 00
New York, Bay Ridge & Jamaica R. R.	525 00
New York Lighterage & Transportation	22 50
New York Ferry	7,730 65
National Transit	20,550 21
Nassau Ferry	1,061 76
New York & Charlestown Steamship	112 50
New York Steam Cable & Towing	17 86

Northern Central	$2,906 82
National Express	2,073 00
Newburgh, Dutchess & Connecticut R. R.	897 28
New York, Woodhaven & Rockaway R. R.	577 64
Newburgh Marine Railway	6 50
New York, Ontario & Western	7,564 25
Olean, Bradford & Warren R. R.	167 57
Oswego & Syracuse R. R.	2,970 90
Ogdensburg & Lake Champlain R. R.	3,221 19
Olean Street R. R.	84 22
Ocean Navigation & Pier	375 00
Panama R. R.	23,625 00
Port Chester Transportation	141 98
Park Avenue R. R.	1 31
Prospect Park & Coney Island R. R.	1,531 62
Perry R. R.	3 00
People's Ferry	583 95
Poughkeepsie Transportation	652 53
Port Jervis & Monticello R. R.	161 58
Port Henry Towing	325 81
Rochester City & Brighton R. R.	1,726 41
Rochester & Lake Ontario R. R.	296 78
Rensselaer & Saratoga R. R.	13,708 20
Rochester Baggage & Transfer	195 14
Rhinebeck & Kingston Ferry	264 94
Rome, Watertown & Ogdensburgh R. R.	9,660 60
Rome & Clinton R. R.	604 28
Rochester & Pittsburgh R. R.	7,328 59
Reed & Powell Transportation	357 90
Rochester & Genesee Valley R. R.	832 80
Romer & Tremper Steamboat	171 22
Rochester & Ontario Belt R. R.	26 24
South Brooklyn Central R. R.	1,173 43
Syracuse & Geddes R. R.	259 06
Steinway & Hunter's Point R. R.	164 85
Sixth Avenue R. R.	6,152 83
Staten Island R. R.	2,443 96
Seneca Lake Steam Navigation	187 77
Schuyler Steam Tow-Boat Line	1,679 35
Saratoga & Schenectady R. R.	787 50
Schoharie Valley R. R.	126 76
Stoney Clove & Catskill Mountain R. R.	266 91
Second Avenue R. R.	8,232 56
Syracuse, Binghamton & New York R. R.	9,416 98
Syracuse & Onondaga R. R.	175 00
Stillwater & Mechanicsville St. R. R.	42 52
Silver Lake R. R.	127 12
Skaneateles R. R.	149 75
Syracuse, Geneva & Corning R. R.	3,567 01
Spuyten Duyvil & Port Morris R. R.	1,978 00
Saratoga, Mt. McGregor & Lake George R. R.	164 02
Sterling Mountain R. R.	188 38
Southfield Branch R. R.	1 75

Syracuse, Ontario & New York R. R.	$377 99
Tonawanda Valley & Cuba R. R.	124 91
Troy & Boston R. R.	2,885 36
Third Avenue R. R.	16,262 03
Troy & Cohoes R. R.	105 00
Troy & Lansingburgh R. R.	1,932 09
Twenty-third Street R. R.	2,575 20
Troy & Albia Horse R. R.	148 34
Troy & Bennington R. R.	226 20
Troy & Greenbush R. R.	480 20
Tehuantepec Inter Ocean R. R.	2 25
Tioga R. R.	202 28
Utica & Mohawk R. R.	27 63
Utica & Black River R. R.	7,194 17
Ulster & Delaware R. R.	1,621 31
Union Steamboat	1,500 00
United Magdalena Steam Navigation	360 00
Utica, Chenango & Susquehanna Valley R. R.	6,000 00
Utica, Clinton & Binghamton R. R.	277 77
Union Ferry	7,449 24
Van Brunt Street & Erie Basin R. R.	98 55
Valley R. R.	956 25
Waverly & State Line R. R.	15 00
Watervliet Turnpike R. R.	547 34
Walkill Valley R. R.	628 88
Washington Street & State Asylum R. R.	35 33
Western Transportation	1,000 00
Zulia Steam Navigation	37 50
	$1,051,946 63

CLASS III.   TELEGRAPH AND TELEPHONE COMPANIES.

Amsterdam Tel. & Teleph.	$16 57
American Dist. Tel. — Troy	131 72
American Dist. Tel. — Brooklyn	578 76
Andes & Delhi Tel.	4 99
American Dist. Tel. —New York	950 93
American Rapid Tel.	225 00
American Dist. Tel.— Syracuse	161 65
American Dist. Tel.— Elmira	13 20
Bell Teleph.	1,799 83
Bankers & Merchants' Tel.	600 00
Central South American Tel.	1 50
Construction Tel. & Teleph.	9 00
Commercial Teleph.—Albany	599 17
Catskill Tel. & Teleph.	3 00
Central New York Tel. & Teleph.	769 17
Commercial Teleph.— Troy	709 76
Capital Dist. Tel.	18 00
Commercial Telegram	46 48
Delhi & Stamford Tel.	1 50

Empire State Tel. & Teleph..........................	$357 95
Eastern Union Tel................................	2 46
East Randolph Teleph.............................	31
Fulton County Teleph.............................	9 75
Gamewell Fire Alarm Tel..........................	112 50
Great North Western Tel...........................	231 39
Holmes Burglar Alarm Tel.........................	112 50
Hudson Tel. & Teleph.............................	7 50
Hudson River Teleph.............................	315 88
Lexington, West Kill & Shandakin Tel.............	2 39
Mutual Union Tel.................................	230 46
Mexican Tel......................................	2 00
Metropolitan Tel. & Teleph.	5,523 06
Mutual Dist. Tel.................................	449 91
New York & Pennsylvania Tel. & Teleph............	306 62
New York Tel....................................	3 00
Northern New York Tel. & Teleph..................	90 00
New York & Vermont Tel. & Teleph................	30 00
New England Tel. & Teleph........................	62
Prospect Park & Coney Island Tel..................	8 75
People's Tel. & Teleph............................	7 50
Postal Tel.......................................	298 10
Southern Tel....................................	150 00
Sandy Hook, Quarantine & City Island Tel..........	25 26
Staten Island Teleph.............................	90 00
Union Tel. & Teleph.............................	253 96

$15,262 10

CLASS IV. GAS, MINING AND MISCELLANEOUS COMPANIES.

Albany Safe Deposit & Storage	$5 00
Albany & Greenbush Bridge.......................	90 00
Argyle & Fort Edward Plankroad..................	14 40
Ansonia Brass & Copper..........................	150 00
Albion Gas-light................................	6 00
American News..................................	2,422 56
Ausable Plankroad...............................	40
Auburn & Fleming Plankroad......................	12 71
Assabet Manufacturing...........................	120 00
American Net & Twine...........................	100 00
Ausable...	7 50
Albany, Schoharie & Rensselaerville Plankroad.....	15 64
Atlantic Dredging...............................	187 50
Avon Water-works...............................	20 70
Albany & Mohawk Plankroad......................	15 00
American Horse Exchange..	105 00
American Whip..................................	45 00
Atlantic Dock...................................	1,500 00
Attica Water-works..............................	90 00
Albany & Sand Lake Plankroad....................	1 02
Albany Gas-light................................	2,187 50

A. E. Smith's Sons Pottery	$13 50
Allegany Oil...	522 50
American Tube Works..............................	225 00
American Dock & Trust............................	785 40
American Bronze Powder Manufacturing............	5 63
Andes Water.......................................	9 75
Auburn Water-works..............................	400 00
American Machinist Publishing	87 50
Amenia Mining......................................	225 00
Attica Salt & Mining..............................	6 12
Amie Mining..	154 50
Amherst Gold Mining	3 75
Auburn Gas-light...................................	300 00
Albany Electric Illuminating......................	379 50
American Eucaustic Tile............................	83 47
Auburn Steam Heating..............................	31 95
Ames Plow..	4 05
Adirondack Placer Mining...........................	5 25
Anchor Oil..	195 00
Associated Fanciers................................	1 13
Atlanta Hill Gold Mining & Milling..................	75 00
Burbank Manufacturing	27 00
Boreel Mining......................................	27 00
Buffalo Loan, Trust & Safe Deposit.................	205 50
Brewers' Ice..	264 39
Brookfield Linen....................................	37 50
Brainard & Armstrong..............................	37 50
Brooklyn Trust.....................................	1,000 00
Brooklyn City Safe Deposit	145 50
Buffalo & Idaho Gold & Silver Mining...............	75 00
Barrett Bridge......................................	31 25
Bigelow Carpet	124 15
Brigham Hall..	250 00
Brabant Plankroad..................................	3 00
Buffalo Board of Trade..............................	70 81
Brooklyn Academy of Music.........................	300 00
Brooklyn Riding Academy...........................	21 00
Brush Electric Light & Power (Niagara Falls)........	15 00
Buffalo Transcript Publishing & Printing............	9 00
Bishop's Derrick & Elevator........................	18 00
Brooklyn Gas-light.................................	5,000 00
Bull Domingo Consolidated Mining..................	15 00
Brockport Gas-light................................	15 00
Buffalo Mutual Gas-light...........................	1,125 00
Buffalo Gas-light...................................	3,000 00
Blue Ridge Clay & Retort...........................	15 00
Bassick Mining.....................................	92 10
Buffalo Herdic Phæton..............................	19 50
Binghamton Gas-light..............................	187 50
Benson Gravel Mining...............................	37 50
Brooklyn Athenæum Reading-room	105 00
Brighton Beach Racing Association..................	37 50

Brush Electric Light (Rochester)........................	$150 00
Belvedere Iron..	37 50
Barcelona Apartment Association	157 50
Brush Electric Light (Buffalo) ...,.................	240 90
Bessemer Mining......................................	13 50
Bankers' Safe Deposit................................	225 00
Belletrisches Journal Publishing.....................	37 50
Buffalo & Rock City Pipe Line........................	649 52
Batavia Gas-light....................................	97 50
Beaton Silver Mining.................................	112 50
Brighton Beach Improvement...........................	67 50
Bridgehampton Beach..................................	30 00
Columbia Turnpike	18 75
Codorus Mining.......................................	37 50
Crystal Company......................................	28 00
Cairo Bridge...	1 29
Central New York Agricultural, Horticultural and Mechanical Association.........................	22 50
Cohoes & Lansingburgh Bridge	61 25
Coeymans & Westerlo Plankroad........................	15 00
Continental Silver Mining............................	24 61
Caryl, Coleman & Co..................................	37 50
Cold Springs Water	1 50
Cheever Ore Bed......................................	250 00
Congress & Empire Springs............................	180 00
Central Trust..	2,000 00
Celluloid Brush......................................	25 00
College Point Gas-light..............................	7 50
Chrysolite Silver Mining.............................	387 00
Consolidated Fruit Jar...............................	1,250 00
Chapman Slate	29 36
Corning Gas-light....................................	33 75
Chateaugay Water-works...............................	14 40
Celluloid Manufacturing..............................	1,406 25
Charlotte Bridge.....................................	3 08
Clinton Wire-cloth...................................	14 01
Catskill & Mountain Turnpike.........................	3 75
Cooperstown Aqueduct Association.....................	1 25
Cherry Valley Creek Plankroad........................	3 00
Canandaigua Gas-light................................	137 50
Citizens' Gas-light, Brooklyn........................	1,800 00
Catskill Mountain House..............................	56 25
Central Gas-light	6,216 00
Cayadutta Plankroad..................................	15 90
China & Japan Trading	4,375 00
Climax Mining	15 00
Chuctanunda Gas-light................................	125 00
Cicero Turnpike	11 50
Columbia Spectator Publishing........................	3 75
Cohoes...	375 00
Cohoes Gas-light.....................................	125 00
Colorado Land & Mining...............................	9 00

9

Central Cafe	$11	25
Citizens' Gas-light, Poughkeepsie	225	00
Citizens' Gas-light, Warsaw	13	82
Citizens' Gas-light, Rochester	57	40
Citizens' Gas-light, Buffalo	525	00
Consumers' Gas-light	300	00
Consumers' Ice	281	25
Central Safe Deposit	28	10
Campbell's Creek Coal	156	69
Coney Island Fuel, Gas & Light	23	30
Columbia & Beaver Silver Mining	92	70
Consolidated Mineral Point Mining	15	00
Cordova Apartment Association	143	25
Clyde Gas-light	22	50
Coalburg Land & Mining	90	00
Charlotte Centre Oil	3	75
Commercial Advertising Association	900	00
Coney Island Jockey Club	1,662	50
Dutchess Turnpike	6	00
Downer Kerosene Oil	15	00
Dolphin Manufacturing	9	00
Davis' Oil	50	00
Dover Stamping	1	50
Delhi Water-works	39	00
Dorchester Union Free Stone	75	00
Deerpark & Minisink Turnpike	6	00
Dolores Valley Mining	154	86
Delaware Turnpike	6	25
Dansville Gas-light	18	75
Dunderburg Mining	22	50
Erie & Atlantic Sleeping Coach	1,973	86
East Aurora Driving Park Association	1	50
Eaton, Cole & Burhans	150	00
Elmira Gas-light	100	00
Elmira Silver Mining	150	00
Export Lumber	750	00
East Albany Gas	37	50
Ellenville Gas-light	18	75
Elmira Water-works	75	00
Eden Musee Grevin Americania	97	50
Edison Electric Light	720	00
Eagle Silver Mining	30	00
Enterprise Transit	75	00
East Chester Gas-light	100	00
East River Gas	69	00
Empire Gas	1,875	00
Essex Mining	30	00
Equitable Mercantile		90
Fulton County Coal	892	50
Fort Miller Bridge	15	00
Fayetteville & Syracuse Plankroad	54	00
Farmers' Hall Association	1	40

Folsom Landing Central Bridge....................	$3 45
Flatbush Plankroad...............................	6 75
Fulton Gas-light.................................	15 90
Flatbush Gas-light...............................	82 50
Fishkill & Matteawan Gas-light....................	7 50
Fort Hunter Suspension Bridge	20 75
Flatbush Water-works.............................	75 00
Fort Edward Water-works..........	47 50
Fulton Municipal Gas.............................	2,189 89
Forest of Deane Iron Ore	1,100 00
Fletcher Gold & Silver Mining....................	7 50
Forest & Stream Publishing.......................	40 50
Frewsburgh Plankroad............................	3 09
Florence Manufacturing..........................	355 18
Fall Brook Coal	150 00
Farmers' Loan & Trust...........................	5,000 00
Fultonville & Johnstown Plankroad	16 87
Franklinville Agricultural & Driving Park Association,	3 75
First National Oil	2 25
Fuller Electrical................................	178 62
Flushing Gas-light...............................	307 50
Great Wyoming Mining	15 45
Greenfield Centre Stock	3 00
Great Western Turnpike..........................	12 59
George T. Patterson Stationary	12 00
Gnome Mining	27 00
Green Island Improvement	285 30
Geneva Gas-light	79 16
Geneseo Gas-light................................	45 00
Gas-light Company of Waverly....................	24 00
Gilbert & Bennett Manufacturing	22 50
Griswoldville Manufacturing......................	24 18
Gouverneur Water-works	12 00
Glens Falls Gas-light.............................	33 00
Glens Falls & Lake George Plankroad	36 00
Georgetown Eureka Mining.......................	37 50
Great Neck Dock.................................	60
Geneva Water-works	30 00
Greenport Wharf	40 50
German-American Loan & Trust	150 00
Gilboa Aqueduct	83
Goshen Gas......................................	7 50
Green Mountain Gold Mining......................	112 50
Gas-light Company of Syracuse	660 00
Gravesend & Coney Island Bridge and Road...........	2 25
Grain Warehousing	120 00
Gardner & Merrill Mining	6 00
Herdic Coach	17 50
Hudson Aqueduct	9 00
Hazard Powder...................................	231 11
Haverstraw Barge................................	7 50
Halfmoon Bridge.................................	36 00

Harlem Gas-light	$2,700 00
Highland & Modena Turnpike	3 65
Hempstead & Jamaica Plankroad	7 65
Hempstead Gas-light	22 50
Hallowell Granite	3 00
Humason & Beckley Manufacturing	10 50
Highland Park Association	1 86
Hortense Mining	53 16
Hidden Treasure Mining	247 50
Haile Gold Mining	22 50
Horn Silver Mining	1,656 96
Hudson River Ice	243 60
Hudson Gas-light	187 56
Homer & Cortland Gas-light	75 00
Harshaw Mining	75 00
Hale & Kilburn Manufacturing	22 50
Hazelwood Oil	250 00
Howe Machine	22 50
Hornellsville Water	46 87
Hall Anderson Gold Mining	15 00
Hoosick Falls Gas-light	375 00
Hempstead Improvement	337 50
Ide & Haverstick	3 00
Iron Silver Mining	2,070 00
International Bridge	1,499 90
Ithaca Water-works	30 00
Ithaca Gas-light	27 19
Ilion & Mohawk Gas-light	67 50
Irine Mill & Mining	4 70
Jay Street & Pool Farm	45
Jessup & Moore Paper	250 00
Jericho Plankroad	9 01
Jamaica Gas-light	60 00
Jamaica & Brooklyn Road	80 61
Jamestown Water Supply	45 00
Jamestown Gas-light	97 50
Kingston Building	12 00
Keeseville & Port Kent Plankroad	3 00
Knickerbocker Gas-light	225 00
Kent Gold Quartz	86 12
Kearsage Silver Mining	30 00
Lake George & Warrensburgh Plankroad	23 06
Lockport & Wright's Corners Plankroad	8 10
Lockport & Warren's Corners Plankroad	18 00
Lake Milk Association	3 00
Lockport & Cambria Plankroad	9 00
Lyons Gas-light	22 40
Little Falls Gas-light	36 15
Lake Street Building Association	25 50
Leadville Consolidated Mining	180 00
Lincoln Safe Deposit	450 00
Long Island Safe Deposit	231 00

Little Pittsburgh Consolidated Mining	$150 00
LeRoy Gas-light	22 50
Lockport Gas-light	200 00
Little Chief Mining	150 00
Lockport Hydraulic	100 32
Live Stock Association	700 63
Lisbon Apartment Association	146 25
Lake Conesus Ice	6 75
Long Island Improvement	900 00
Long Island Home Hotel	90 00
Lyons Driving Park Association	2 36
Manhattan Beach Improvement	977 79
Monitor Mining	9 00
Marshall Basin Mining	7 20
Metropolitan Concert	22 50
Moresville Turnpike	3 00
Metropolitan Gas-light, New York	12,500 00
Metropolitan Gas-light, Brooklyn	1,304 85
Middletown & Delhi Turnpike	9 37
Meriden Britannia	2,475 00
Malone Water-works	87 50
Mercantile Trust	4,000 00
Maynard Chemical	8 25
Morris & Cumings Dredging	187 50
Malone Gas-light	10 18
Mercantile Safe Deposit	1,762 50
Manlius & Delphi Plankroad	8 12
Middletown & Wurtsboro Turnpike	12 00
Monticello & Wurtsboro Turnpike	7 59
Meriden Cutlery	8 00
Mason & Hamlin Organ and Piano	56 00
Manlius Plankroad	34 67
Manhattan Real Estate Association	1,125 00
Manhattan Shipping	156 25
Minden Gas-light	52 50
Middletown Gas-light	30 00
Meriden Malleable Iron	9 00
Morris Land	450 00
Monticello & White Lake Turnpike	13 75
Metropolitan Trust	1,800 00
Medina & Alabama Plankroad	10 12
Mapes Formula & Peruvian Guano	175 00
Metropolitan Steamship	1,875 00
Municipal Gas-light, Rochester	300 00
Mount Hope Iron	22 50
Middleburgh Bridge	34 38
Mining Record Printing & Publishing	7 50
Manhattan Gas	25,000 00
Moultrie Mining	18 00
Municipal Gas, New York	11,250 00
Metropolitan Gas Saving	12 15
Mohawk Valley Hotel	30 00

Minas Prietas Mining....................................	$37 50
Moose River Improvement..............................	08
Montauk Gas Coal.....................................	6 38
Metropolitan Opera House.............................	1,575 00
Manhattan Beach Bathing.............................	93 75
Montauk Association..................................	22 50
Mizzentop	24 00
Medina Gas-light	22 50
Mutual District Messenger............................	11 25
Mahopac Iron Ore	150 00
Manhattan Polo Association	21 00
Madrid Apartment Association	192 75
Mirror Newspaper	4 50
Municipal Gas, Yonkers..............................	46 61
Mutual Benefit Ice Co., New York....................	112 50
New York Central Sleeping Car	6,599 69
Niagara Falls International Bridge....................	1,625 00
New York Supply & Equipment	1 50
Niagara River Bridge	18 80
New York Cattle	107 81
New Haven Clock	37 50
Neuchatel Asphalt.	30 00
Nassau Gas-light.....................................	750 00
Nasshauannuck Manufacturing.........................	13 50
Northampton Cutlery	9 45
Nonotuck Silk..	180 00
National Mining & Exploring..........................	30 00
New York Stock Exchange Building....................	1,050 00
New York Steam Dredging	197 00
Niagara Falls Suspension Bridge	172 50
New York Floating Elevator..........................	151 87
Northern Gas-light...................................	150 00
New York Real Estate Association....................	2,000 00
Narrowsburgh Bridge	3 60
New York Safety Steam Power........................	18 00
New York City Ice..	187 27
Niagara Falls Gas....................................	75 84
New Paltz Turnpike	26 25
New York Warehousing................................	240 00
Niagara Grape	12 00
New York, New England & Western Investment......	3 00
New York Gas-light..................................	10,000 00
Nassau Trading	30 00
New York Coal Tar & Chemical.......................	825 00
New York Cafe.......................................	4 50
Navassa Phosphate...................................	105 00
Niagara Falls Water-works............................	80 00
New York Steam Power...............................	150 00
New York Guaranty & Indemnity	411 86
New York Mutual Gas-light	8,750 00
New York Floating Dry Dock.........................	210 00
Niagara Falls Prospect Park	384 37

North Hemstead & Flushing Turnpike and Bridge	$7 32
New York & Coney Island Observatory and Signal.....	90 00
New Haven Copper	20 00
North Am. Attorneys & Tradesmen Protective Union..	47 93
New York Loan & Improvement	1,800 00
New York & New Jersey Globe Gas-light	5 70
National Ice...	337 50
New York Dairy.......................................	18 00
Niagara Falls Hydraulic Power & Manufacturing......	97 50
National Mining.......................................	22 50
New York & Silver Peak Mining	15 00
New York & Palmetto Mining	30 00
Nyack Water-works	150 00
National Sleeping Car.................................	12 00
Newburgh & Cochecton Turnpike Road	4 52
Newburgh & New Windsor Turnpike Road............	7 35
New York Stock.......................................	15 00
Oneida Gas-light.......................................	18 75
Oswego Water-works	167 70
Oswego Canal	102 50
Oneonta Water-works	62 40
Oysterman's Dock.....................................	3 60
Oneonta & Franklin Turnpike	5 30
Ogdensburg Coal & Towing...........................	91 85
Orient Wharf	21 00
Ogdensburg Gas-light..................................	75 00
Oswego Railroad Bridge	131 25
Our Home Hygienic Institution	90 00
Oneida Street Lighting	22 50
Oswego Gas-light......................................	279 05
Otter Gulch Mining...................................	15 00
Owego Gas-light.......................................	70 95
Oswego Normal School Boarding House	8 10
Owego Water-works...................................	7 50
Owyhee Gold & Silver Mining.......................	3 00
Oneida Block..	11 14
Producers' Consolidated Land & Petroleum..........	175 82
Patent Water & Gas Pipe............................	10 64
Pennsylvania Coal.....................................	2,917 08
Poughkeepsie Gas-light	147 00
Purdy & Huntington..................................	15 00
Produce Exchange Cold Warehousing	100 00
Peekskill Gas-light....................................	46 50
Port Henry Gas-light..................................	5 10
Penderry Mining......................................	1 43
Penn Yan Gas-light....................................	27 84
Port Jervis Gas-light..................................	40 00
Port Jervis Water-works...............................	81 00
Prince Manufacturing.................................	54 00
Pre-emption Park......................................	4 50
People's Gas-light (Albany)	100 00
Palmyra Gas-light.....................................	30 00

Port Henry Iron Ore	$7,750	00
Peck Brothers & Co	35	00
Putnam County Ice	18	75
Porter's Corners Mercantile Association	26	50
People's Gas-light (Brooklyn)	.757	50
Piety Hill Gold & Silver Mining	135	93
Pawling & Beekman Turnpike	7	62
Passaic Chemical	58	50
Prospect Park Hotel	75	36
Plattsburgh Gas	15	00
Peters & Calhoun	12	50
Peck, Stow & Wilcox	562	50
Putnam Machine	6	18
Port Royal Fertilizer	52	50
Photo Engraving	30	00
Pleasure Island	9	75
Quincy Mining	475	00
Quicksilver Mining	3,143	56
Rensselaer & Columbia Turnpike	7	20
Rexford Flats Bridge	5	25
Russell Erwin Manufactory	1,875	00
Rome Turnpike	1	50
Remmington Sewing Machine	90	00
Richmondville & Summit Plankroad	1	92
Rye & Port Chester Gas-light	37	50
Revere Copper	37	50
Real Estate Trust	450	00
Rome Gas	70	00
Rock City Mining & Manufacturing	150	00
Rondout & Kingston Gas-light	113	75
Rochester Gas-light	1,225	00
Rochester Driving Park Association	176	25
Ridgewood Ice	210	00
Retail Dealers' Protective Association	42	17
Rockaway Beach Pier	2	25
Rochester & Charlotte Turnpike Road	12	00
Richardson Gold & Silver Mining	37	50
Rochester & Hemlock Lake Plankroad	6	70
Richmond County Gas-light	566	56
Rochester & Pittsford Plankroad	1	51
Rollins Gold & Silver Mining	75	00
Rochester Electric Light	17	91
Rhinebeck Gas	7	50
Ruby Silver Mining	3	00
Richmond Gravel Mining	3	75
Red Elephant Mining	37	50
Rochester & Gates Plankroad	17	88
South Yuba Water & Mining	4,289	40
South Bethlehem Plankroad	3	16
Stamford Manufacturing	300	00
Sturges Elevator	93	75
Syracuse Water	660	00
Shelter Island Park Association	16	87

Small Hopes Mining..	$37 50
Sandy Hill & Adamsville Plankroad..................	14 80
Southport Plankroad	26 70
Susquehanna Turnpike	26 1(
Saratoga Vichy Springs.............................	100 00
Southern Tier Mining..............................	30 00
Syracuse & Dumont Consol, Mining.................	2 12
Safe Deposit, New York...........................	424 95
Sidney Bridge	3 60
Saratoga Gas-light	60 00
Sodus Bay Elevator	90 00
Stationers' Board of Trade	3 75
Sandy Hill Quarry	400 00
Schenectady Water.................................	112 50
Schenectady Gas-light..............................	75 00
South Yuba Mining and Tunnel.....................	15 00
Syracuse & Jamesville Plankroad....................	16 58
Sag Harbor & Bulls-head Turnpike..................	2 02
Stamford Water....................................	17 28
Stillwater & Schaghticoke Bridge...................	31 02
Spring Valley Hydraulic Gold......................	300 00
Sing Sing Gas Manufacturing.......................	33 75
Stuyvesant Safe Deposit	350 00
Saratoga Springs...................................	6 00
Sarato a Lake Bridge	6 00
Sidney& Unadilla Bridge...........................	7 39
Safe Deposit (Rochester)..........................	135 00
Schuylerville Bridge.........	22 50
Seneca Falls & Waterloo Gas-light..................	120 00
Salamanca Water-works	15 00
Star Rubber	106 43
Salina & Central Square Plankroad	74 31
Senate Mining & Smelting..........................	15 00
Syracuse & Liverpool...............................	7 50
Saratoga Association for Improvement of Breed of Horses.	87 50
Saugerties Gas-light...............................	80 00
Seymour Paper....................................	168 75
Schenevus Water...................................	1 20
Saranac Plankroad.................................	56 77
St. Joseph Lead .,.................................	975 00
Socialistic Co-operative Publishing.................	3 28
Staten Island Publishing...........................	9 00
Troy & West Troy Bridge...........................	150 75
Ticonderoga Water-works...........................	32 50
Troy Gas-light....................................	525 00
Tilley Foster Iron Mines...........................	750 00
Troy & Sandlake Turnpike	75 00
Tide-Water Pipe...................................	966 38
Thousand Islands Park Association..................	52 50
Troy Citizens' Gas	79 00
Tarrytown & Irvington Union Gas-light.............	90 00
United States Express.............................	541 95

10

Union Bridge	$200	00
United States Trust	11,250	00
Utica Water-works	600	00
University Publishing	7	87
Utica Gas-light	400	00
Union Trust	2,125	00
United States Mortgage	750	00
Union Plankroad	7	50
Union Stock Yards and Market	500	00
Ulster Spinning	37	50
United States Warehouse	254	02
Unadilla Valley Stock Breeders' Association	15	00
United Pipe Line	4,728	12
Universal Button-hole Attachment	9	00
United States Rolling Stock	1,774	18
Union Wharf	6	00
Universal Beer Keg	1	80
Union Horse Society of Ulster County		19
United States Mercantile Reporting	75	00
Union Gas-light	262	50
Vulcan Gold & Silver Mining	4	50
Warburton Hall Association	47	50
Waterville Opera House	12	37
Washington Park Association	9	00
W. Jessup & Sons	75	00
West Troy Gas-light	187	50
Warrensburgh & Chester Plankroad and Turnpike		27
Western Plankroad	7	11
Waverly Water	30	00
Winchester Repeating Arms	155	00
Warwick Valley Farmers' Milk Association	91	20
Watertown Gas-light	150	00
Walton Water-works	22	50
Woodside Mining	7	50
Whitehall & Granville Turnpike	1	92
Williamsburgh Gas-light	1,125	00
West Troy Water-works	37	50
White Plains Gas	50	00
Warsaw Water	30	38
Weed Iron	15	00
Washington Building	1,050	00
Whitehall Gas-light	12	00
Wilcox Silver Plate	34	00
Waldron Consolidated Silver Mining	37	50
Walter Haywood Chair	18	00
West Jamaica Land	75	00
Wood River Smelting	80	55
York Street Flax Spinning	37	50
Yonkers Gas-light	300	37
Yedras Mining	562	50
	$251,069	96

CLASS V. BANKS.

Agency Bank of Montreal — New York	$22,266 58
Agency Bank of British North America..............	7,437 81
Agency Merchants' Bank of Canada.................	4,362 17
Canadian Bank of Commerce.......................	3,254 35
	$37,320 91

RECAPITULATION.

Class I. Insurance...............................	$248,013 15
Class II. Transportation..........................	1,051,946 63
Class III. Telegraph and Telephone.................	15,262 10
Class IV. Gas, Mining and Miscellaneous............	251,069 96
Class V. Banks...................................	37,320 91
	$1,603,612 75

Payments, Account Construction New Capitol

October, 1883:

Pay-roll, Sept. 28. Labor and team work............. $41,261 36
     28. Commissioner and clerks.......... 852 72
   Oct. 12. Labor and team work. 42,717 97
     12. Commissioner and clerks.......... 846 86
     19. Labor........................... 1,035 86
     26. Labor and team work............. 37,369 89
     26. Commissioner and clerks.. .... 753 86
Eidlitz, Richardson & Co., architects 1,666 66

Fuel, Freight, Dock Rent, Stationery, etc.

Blackburn & Jones....................................... 243 27
Albany Gas-light Co.................................... 94 55
The Argus Co. 41 50
E. Bicknell........ .... 16 00
E. Ellis & Co.. 54 35
W. E. Peck 36 70
Albany Morning Express 20 25
John Switzer.. 110 25
Thos. Lynch 112 45
Hudson River Bridge Co............................. 100 59
John Mullon 55 08
E. W. Sewell.. 19 92
Commercial Telephone Co............................ 4 00
Albany Railway.. 835 25

Stone, Brick, Cement, Sand, etc.

Peter McCabe 622 05
Wm. Fuller & Son 40 50
Peter McCabe... 69 30
L. C. Woodruff.... .... 8 75
Wasson & Martin 143 61
Bodwell Granite Co 10,898 70

S. Klaber & Co.	$807 82
S. Klaber & Co.	2,070 00
Jas. C. Moore.	965 07
Thos. McCarty	244 12
Howe's Cave Association	235 58
Wm. Manson	330 00
Johnson & Wilson	235 00

Iron, Steel, Hardware, Tools, Plumbing, etc.

Corning & Co.	815 03
Sullivan & Ehlers.	2,622 51
Breslin Bros.	72 20
M. E. Viele	102 60
Albany Steam Trap Co	16 00
M. Delehanty & Son	2,361 05
Sullivan & Ehlers.	2,096 76
Sullivan & Ehlers.	78 20
Sullivan & Ehlers.	117 80
Sullivan & Ehlers.	1,901 11

Lumber and Woodwork.

Thos. Murphy.	379 14
J. O. Towner & Co.	706 91
Van Santford & Eaton	182 00
L. Brainerd	33 00
J. J. Weller.	7,000 00

Paints, Oils, Glass, Rope, etc.

R. B. Wing.	359 78
D. H. Fonda & Co.	·796 63
A. McClure & Co.	2 86
A. Groesbeck	6 50
Semon Bache & Co.	,220 00

South-east Staircase.

James Sinclair & Co.	20,000 00

Total for October, 1883	$185,789 83

November, 1883:

Pay-roll, Nov. 9. Labor and team work	$36,003 33
9. Commissioner and clerks	822 27
17. Labor	964 45
23. Labor and team work	29,083 62
23. Commissioner and clerks	823 36
Eidlitz, Richardson & Co., architects.	1,666 66

Fuel, Transportation, Stationery, etc.

E. Ellis & Co.	26 83
The Argus Co.	31 50
Commercial Telephone Co.	5 00

James Mahar	$1 30
Albany Railway Co.	616 63
Thos. Lynch	135 90
John Switzer	136 80
J. Smith & Son	126 71
Jno. Mullon	13 92
J. & J. Doran	40
Johnson & Reilly	14 00
John Switzer	41 50
E. W. Sewell	134 71
Blackburn & Jones	275 65
Patrick Shevlin	6 10

Stone, Brick, Cement, Sand, Marble and Mosaic Work, etc.

Peter McCabe	83 16
Peter McCabe	324 82
C. L. Woodruff	3 50
Johnson & Wilson	235 00
James C. Moore	672 55
Thos. McCarty	185 63
Howe's Cave Association	237 04
Bodwell Granite Co.	5,731 12
Wm. Manson	226 00
S. Klaber & Co	386 00
A. D. Person	1,377 00
Wasson & Martin	1,245 16
Robt. C. Fisher	408 95
A. S. Nichols & Co.	1,491 66
Johnson & Wilson	235 00
Eaglesen & De Veau	214 76
William Manson	4,000 00

Iron, Steel, Hardware, Tools, Plumbing, etc.

M. E. Viele	72 16
Breslin Bros.	38 88
Corning & Co.	675 12
W. H. D. Sweet, agent	33 56
F. R. McName & Bro.	223 15
Cook, Rymes & Co.	4 00
M. Delehanty & Son	2,553 77
Sullivan & Ehlers	7,500 00
J. Chevally	32 00
Sullivan & Rice	683 70
Sullivan & Ehlers	314 00
J. & W. Rothery	21 87
Sullivan & Ehlers	301 05
Sullivan & Ehlers	417 62
Sullivan & Ehlers	211 27

Paints, Oils, Glass, Rope, Covering Steam Pipes, etc.

E. Bicknell	$7 00
W. E. Peck	46 00
Wasson & Martin	38 22
D. H. Fonda & Co	723 83
J. & W. Covell	85 00
Mayer & Lowenstein	30 60
R. B. Wing	248 80
P. J. Nolan	3 00
John Palmer	115 50
Albany Steam Planing Mill	3 00
Riley Brothers	1,279 74

Lumber, Cabinet Work and Models.

LaRose & Lavelly	243 26
Evans & Tombs	5,648 95
Thomas Murphy	19 69
J. O. Towner & Co	1,199 51
Van Santford & Eaton	51 30

Total for November, 1883	$110,813 54

December, 1883 :

Pay-roll, Dec. 7. Labor and team work	$24,179 70
7. Commissioner and clerks	820 36
14. Labor	1,390 61
21. Labor and team work	19,870 00
21. Commissioner and clerks	826 56
Eidlitz, Richardson & Co., architects	1,666 66

Fuel, Transportation, Stationery, etc.

E. Ellis & Co	68 67
The Argus Co	41 00
Commercial Telephone Co	5 00
Albany Railway	828 00
Thomas Lynch	54 90
John Switzer	116 98
Blackburn & Jones	265 98
Ellen T. Tobin, executrix	45 00
John Smith	45 17
John Mullon	8 88
Albany City Water-works	366 83
E. W. Sewell	15 34

Stone, Cement, Sand, Lime, etc.

Peter McCabe	55 44
Peter McCabe	102 25
James C. Moore	296 78
Thomas McCarty	182 25
Howe's Cave Association	193 31

Bodwell Granite Co $7,806 00
O. D. Person.. 581 40
S. Klaber & Co..................................... 1,413 40
Wasson & Martin.................................... 185 00
Wasson & Martin.................................... 3,223 32

Iron, Steel, Hardware, Tools, etc.

Sullivan & Ehlers................................... 1,759 48
M. E. Viele.. 22 74
Peter Kinnear...................................... 10 05
Corning & Co....................................... 377 71
Shields Brothers 12 03
Abendroth & Root Manufacturing Co................. 20 27
Sullivan & Ehlers.................................. 505 48
Sullivan & Ehlers.................................. 1,058 53
Sullivan & Ehlers.................................. 223 61
Sullivan & Ehlers.................................. 60 00
Sullivan & Ehlers.................................. 291 20
Sullivan & Ehlers.................................. 131 65
M. Delehanty & Son................................ 3,080 27
Sullivan & Ehlers.................................. 6,000 00

Lumber and Wood Work.

George H. Cheney................................... 234 00
Thomas Murphy..................................... 692 18
J. O. Towner & Co.................................. 1,107 13
J. K. Benway 3 75

Paints, Oils, Glass, Rope, etc.

D. H. Fonda & Co................................... 790 09
Robert Geer.. 1 59
R. B. Wing... 274 15
J. & J. Doran...................................... 3 00
Johnston & Reilly.................................. 28 00
A. E. Rendle 2,000 00

South-east Staircase.

James Sinclair & Co................................ 25,000 00

Total for December, 1883..................... $108,342 70

January, 1884 :
Pay-roll, Jan. 4. Labor and team work.............. $15,918 72
                4. Commissioner and clerks........... 817 31
                7. Labor 213 55
               11. Labor 2,500 77
               18. Labor and team work............. 10,790 58
               18. Commissioner and clerks......... 852 86
Eidlitz, Richardson & Co., architects................ 1,666 66

11

Fuel, Transportation, Repair, Machinery, Stationery, etc.

W. I. Norwood	$200 00
Thos. Lynch	48 30
John Switzer	76 05
Blackburn & Jones	417 37
The Argus Co	10 50
E. Ellis & Co	15 05
E. W. Sewell	48 24
Albany Railway	241 02
Albany Gas-light Co	65 75
Commercial Telephone Co	5 00
Sullivan & Ehlers	498 00
Sullivan & Ehlers	144 00
Sullivan & Ehlers	306 00

Stone, Brick, Cement, Sand, Marble Work, etc.

William Manson	4,000 00
Johnson & Wilson	235 00
Chas. E. Lee	150 00
James C. Moore	621 42
Thos. McCarty	165 37
Peter McCabe	140 87
Bodwell Granite Co	1,472 38
Howe's Cave Association	274 01
Wasson & Martin	2,689 20
A. S. Nichols & Co.	1,016 16
Peter McCabe	41 58

Iron, Steel, Hardware, Tools, Plumbing, etc.

M. Delehanty & Son	1,937 40
J. & W. Covell	42 50
Patrick Shevlin	16 50
Shields Brothers	16 12
Patrick Kinnear	531 56
Corning & Co.	470 58
M. E. Viele	17 18
Breslin Brothers	33 90
Wasson & Martin	1,234 00
Sullivan & Ehlers	5,000 00
Sullivan & Ehlers	89 60
Sullivan & Ehlers	583 41
Sullivan & Ehlers	176 83
Sullivan & Ehlers	432 15
Sullivan & Ehlers	171 87
Sullivan & Ehlers	1,411 62
Sullivan & Ehlers	683 29
Sullivan & Ehlers	198 62

Lumber and Wood Work.

Thos. Murphy	522 58
Evans & Tombs	1,274 66
J. J. Weller	2,785 76

Paints, Glass, Varnish, Rope, Work on Skylight, etc.

A. E. Rendle	$2,200 00
J. W. Eaton & Co.	60 25
H. Mayell & Son	10 80
D. H. Fonda & Co.	373 48
R. B. Wing	225 87
J. & J. Doran	11 75
Johnston & Reilly	3 50
Morton Havens	28 00
Total for January, 1884	$66,185 50

February, 1884 :

Pay-roll, Feb. 1. Labor and team work	$1,060 51
1. Commissioner and clerks	798 70
15. Labor and team work	835 32
15. Commissioner and clerks	809 08
A. E. Rendle, account, skylight	20 00
Total for February, 1884	$3,523 61

March, 1884 :

Pay-roll, Feb. 29. Labor and team work	$941 15
29. Commissioner and clerks	803 23
March 14. Labor and team work	867 60
14. Commissioner and clerks	793 46
28. Labor and team work	10,089 36
28. Commissioner and clerks	829 46

Fuel, Dock Rent, Stationery, etc.

Hudson River Bridge Co.	100 50
John Switzer	38 20
Edwin Ellis & Co.	28 85
Commercial Telephone Co.	10 00
Albany Gas-light Co.	45 00
Blackburn & Jones	212 10
E. W. Sewell	85 82
Thomas Lynch	13 95

Terra Cotta, Brick, Tile and Sand.

James C. Moore	189 96
Orrin D. Person	2,000 00
Orrin D. Person	731 00
Thomas McCarty	40 50
Orrin D. Person	2,000 00

Iron, Steel, Hardware, Tools, Iron Work, Plumbing, etc.

Corning & Co.	409 37
M. E. Viele	1 80

W. G. Creamer & Co....................................	$598 94
Sullivan & Ehlers.....................................	18,000 00
Nason Manufacturing Company.....................	154 85
M. Delehanty & Son.................................	1,476 28

Lumber.

Thomas Murphy......................................	144 73

Sundries.

D. H. Fonda & Co....................................	121 28
Johnston & Reilly	1 75
A. C. Rendle..	1,800 00

South-east Staircase.

James Sinclair & Co	25,000 00
Total for March, 1884........................	$67,529 14

April, 1884 :

Pay-roll, April 11. Labor and team work.............	$32,829 76
11. Commissioner and clerks..........	872 85
25 Labor and team work.............	39,500 16
25. Commissioner and clerks..........	872 87
Eidlitz, Richardson & Co., for January................	1,666 66
Eidlitz, Richardson & Co., for February..............	1,666 66

Fuel, Dock Rent, Stationery, etc.

Breslin Brothers.....................................	34 33
Hudson River Bridge Company.................... ...	100 50
Edwin Ellis & Co....................................	59 35
Commercial Telephone Company....................	5 00
I. G. Perry	35 99
The Argus Company..................................	19 50
Robert Jones..	6 00
Blackburn & Jones	173 71

Stone, Bricks, Cement, Encaustic Tiling, Marble Work, etc.

James C. Moore	208 75
S. Klaber & Co......................................	822 28
Johnson & Wilson	72 50
R. C. Fisher..	1,491 77
Thomas McCarty.....................................	279 31
James C. Moore.....................................	1,047 29
Howe's Cave Association.............................	494 38
A. S. Nichols & Co..................................	1,536 00
Johnson & Wilson	236 00
James Sinclair & Co.................................	2,097 29
Johnson & Wilson	246 00

Iron, Iron Work, Steel, Hardware, Tools, Plumbing, etc.

Corning & Co	$453 79
Wasson & Martin	391 01
M. Delehanty & Son	182 68
Sullivan & Ehlers	3,425 20
Sullivan & Ehlers	435 27
Sullivan & Ehlers	811 14
Sullivan & Ehlers	377 08
Caledonian Tool Works	41 00
Sullivan & Ehlers	235 40

Lumber.

Thomas Murphy	334 80

South-east Staircase.

James Sinclair & Co	25,000 00

Sundries — Slating Roof, Covering Pipes, Varnish, Oils, Carpets, etc.

D. H. Fonda & Co	208 18
R. B. Wing	63 45
Van Heusen, Charles & Co	142 40
La Rose & Laveilly	18 00
R. B. Wing	48 00
W. M. Whitney	3,704 35
W. M. Whitney	870 00
George Tolmire	111 00
Wasson & Martin	5,907 12
Wasson & Martin	290 84
Total for April, 1884	$129,425 61

May, 1884 :

Pay-roll, May 9. Labor and team work	$41,356 86
9. Commissioner and clerks	868 82
23. Labor and team work	41,598 91
23. Commissioner and clerks	865 46

Fuel, Stationery, etc.

Edwin Ellis & Co	51 60
The Argus Company	51 62
Commercial Telephone Company	5 00
Blackburn & Jones	113 72
I. G. Perry	35 39

Tile, Marble Work, Cement, etc.

Peter McCabe	527 90
James C. Moore	544 91

Howe's Cave Association	$372	41
S. Klaber & Co	368	00
Peter McCabe	76	23
Wm. Manson	224	83
John Switzer	99	84
Wm. Manson	2,036	10

Iron, Iron Work, Steel, Hardware, Tools, Plumbing, etc.

W. H. D. Sweet, agent	32	04
Townsend Furnace	348	55
Van Heusen, Charles & Co	2	00
M. E. Viele	59	43
M. Delehanty & Son	493	55
Corning & Co	890	70
Sullivan & Ehlers	835	94
Sullivan & Ehlers	56	50
Sullivan & Ehlers	175	78
Sullivan & Ehlers	383	78
Sullivan & Ehlers	885	66
George Tolmire	7	00
Sullivan & Ehlers	886	77
Sullivan & Rice	1,176	85
Sullivan & Ehlers	4,086	02

Lumber.

Thomas Murphy	933	52
Sullivan & Ehlers	125	95
J. O. Towner & Co	5,008	28

South-east Staircase.

James Sinclair & Co	25,000	00

Sundries, Oils, Glass, Mirrors, Rope, etc.

A. McClure & Co	275	00
Lansing & Co	62	36
Henry Mayell & Son	26	25
Robert Geer	16	22
R. B. Wing	198	36
J. & J. Doran	29	20
D. H. Fonda & Co	393	18
A. Van Allen, Jr	10	00
E. A. Boyd & Son	586	76
A. E. Rendle	1,439	46

Total for May, 1884	$133,622	71

June, 1884:

Pay-roll, June	6.	Labor and team work	$37,965	85
	6.	Commissioner and clerks	870	00
	20.	Labor and team work	41,519	13
	20.	Commissioner and clerks	874	87

Fuel, Gas, Stationery, etc.

J. & J. Doran	$1 50
Edwin Ellis & Co.	15 06
The Argus Company	7 00
James Maher	1 00
Commercial Telephone Company	5 00
Albany Morning Express	40 50
Blackburn & Jones	186 40
I. G. Perry	21 35
Albany Gas-light Company	51 00

Stone, Terra Cotta, Marble, Cement, etc.

Peter McCabe	100 80
Peter McCabe	288 70
Wasson & Martin	250 46
Johnson & Wilson	135 50
James C. Moore	212 67
Howe's Cave Association	256 73
John Switzer	147 65
T. S. Coolidge	49 05
Peter McCabe	80 85
James Sinclair & Co.	2,144 18
Thomas Lynch	11 76
Orrin D. Person	2,150 00
Robert C. Fisher	406 68
Johnson & Wilson	256 00
Thomas Reilly	4 74

Iron, Iron Work, Hardware, Tools, Plumbing, etc.

Breslin Bros.	47 55
W. H. D. Sweet, agent	15 16
Peter Kinnear	30 10
Corning & Co.	880 09
Sullivan & Ehlers	3,694 66
Sullivan & Ehlers	29 00
Sullivan & Ehlers	272 88
Sullivan & Ehlers	48 00
M. Delehanty & Son	270 68

Lumber and Wood Work.

J. O. Towner & Co.	925 11
La Rose Manufacturing Co.	11 25
Thomas Murphy	690 25

South-east Staircase.

James Sinclair & Co.	25,000 00

Sundries, Oils, Paints, Rope, Clocks, Upholstering, etc.

R. B. Wing	190 85
D. H. Fonda & Co.	371 63

John G. Myers	$274 50
Ithaca Calendar Clock Co...........................	278 00
Binghamton Oil Refining Co.........................	70 33
Johnson & Coventry	29 25
Total for June, 1884	$121,173 72

July, 1884.

Pay-roll, July 4. Labor and team work..............	$28,980 76
4. Commissioner and clerks...........	872 18
18. Labor............................	15,568 34
18. Labor and team work..............	29,386 25
18. Commissioner and clerks...........	865 46

Fuel, Rent of Engine, Transportation, etc.

Edwin Ellis & Co................................. •	20 30
The Argus Co......................................	18 50
Commercial Telephone Co...........................	5 00
Albany Railway....................................	355 00
Blackburn & Jones.................................	178 60
Sullivan & Ehlers.................................	200 00

Stone, Brick, Cement, Sand, etc.

Bodwell Granite Co................................	4,722 43
Peter McCabe......................................	86 40
Peter McCabe......................................	313 05
Johnson & Wilson..................................	256 00
Jas. C. Moore.....................................	176 22
Howe's Cave Association............................	210 18
John Switzer......................................	118 18
T. S. Coolidge & Co...............................	117 72
A. S. Nichols	280 00
Johnson & Wilson..................................	54 20

Iron, Iron Work, Hardware, Tools, Electric Light Machines, etc.

Sullivan & Ehlers.................................	3,221 43
M. Delehanty & Son................................	555 60
Corning & Co......................................	341 72
Bates & Johnson...................................	1,455 72
Sullivan & Ehlers.................................	625 40
Sullivan & Ehlers.................................	1,500 00
Sullivan & Ehlers.................................	135 03
W. H. Ely	570 00
Sullivan & Ehlers.................................	585 13
Sullivan & Ehlers.................................	436 05
Sullivan & Ehlers.................................	82 97
Sullivan & Ehlers.................................	892 43
Sullivan & Ehlers.................................	29 82
Sullivan & Ehlers.................................	55 57

Sullivan & Ehlers...............................	$89	20
W. H. Jackson.................................	290	90
Sullivan & Ehlers..............................	4,545	71

Lumber.

Wm. Burton's Sons	49	69
J. O. Towner & Co.............................	222	39
Thos. Murphy.................................	516	28
Jno. W. Hoyt.................................	22	40

South-east Staircase.

James Sinclair & Co............................	25,000	00

Sundries — Rope, Paints, Oils, Glass, etc.

Breslin Bros	44	76
Wasson & Martin	74	46
A. Van Allen, Jr..............................	1	25
Robert Geer..................................	2	65
R. B. Wing	368	60
D. H. Fonda & Co..............................	393	77
La Rose Manufacturing Co.......................	18	00
S. & P. Templeton	7	25
Flynn Bros...................................	20	00
I. G. Perry..................................	43	29
W. J. Norwood...............................	100	00
Jno. Mullon..................................	33	60
Jno. Palmer.................................	6	00
Total for July, 1884..........................	$125,121	84

August, 1884:

Pay-roll, Aug. 1. Labor and team work.	$26,804	86
1. Commissioner and clerks..........	865	46
15. Labor and team work.............	27,761	40
15. Commissioner and clerks..........	865	46
Eidlitz, Richardson & Co., architects	4,542	99

Fuel, Dock Rent, Stationery, etc.

The Argus Co	34	00
S. H. Lloyd Co...............................	12	80
Commercial Telephone Co.......................	5	00
Thomas Lynch	7	50
Hudson River Bridge Co	100	50
Blackburn & Jones............................	194	21
I. G. Perry..................................	20	34
John Mullon.................................	19	00
Edwin Ellis & Co..............................	30	95

Stone, Brick, Cement, Marble, etc.

Eaglesen & De Veau	239	10
Johnson & Wilson	256	00

James C. Moore....................................	$155 60
Howe's Cave Association............................	214 41
John Switzer......................................	137 70
T. S. Coolidge....................................	83 39
Peter McCabe.....................................	43 20
James Sinclair & Co	247 95
Peter McCabe	228 75
Johnson & Wilson.................................	256 00
S. Klaber & Co....................................	345 53
G. P. Sherwood, agent.............................	3,338 40
Bodwell Granite Co...............................	8,384 30
F. G. Clark	1,833 31

Iron, Iron Work, Hardware, Tools, Steam and Gas Fittings, etc.

Sullivan & Ehlers.................................	3,971 81
Sullivan & Ehlers.................................	1,066 17
Sullivan & Ehlers.................................	16 80
Breslin Bros......................................	17 40
Townsend Furnace	3 50
Sullivan & Ehlers.................................	810 24
Jno. W. Hoyt.....................................	25 70
M. Delehanty & Son...............................	846 70
Corning & Co	465 65
Bates & Johnson..................................	3,301 34
United States Reflector Co.........................	1,064 59
Sullivan & Ehlers.................................	148 76
Sullivan & Ehlers.................................	148 32
Sullivan & Ehlers.................................	2,041 99
Sullivan & Ehlers.................................	994 85

Lumber.

Wm. Burton's Sons	57 74
Thos. Murphy....................................	366 14
J. O. Towner	1,349 49

South-east Staircase.

| James Sinclair & Co .... | 25,000 00 |

Sundries — Paints, Oils, Rope, etc.

John Palmer.....................................	48 30
H. Mayell & Son	2 53
Wasson & Martin.................................	120 25
R. B. Wing	47 54
Johnson & Reilly	1 00
W. M. Whitney & Co	3 75
D. H. Fonda & Co	355 44
S. & P. Templeton................................	3 45

| Total for August, 1884......................... | $119,307 56 |

September, 1884:

Pay-roll, Aug. 29. Labor and team work............	$27,897	15
29. Commissioner and clerks..........	835	46
Sept. 12. Labor and team work............	28,262	06
12. Commissioner and clerks..........	802	20
26. Labor and team work............	29,948	48
26. Commissioner and clerks..........	856	86
Eidlitz, Richardson & Co., architects.................	833	33

Fuel, Transportation, Stationery, etc.

Edwin Ellis & Co....................................	31	70
The Argus Co......................................	16	50
Commercial Telephone Co...........................	5	00
Blackburn & Jones.................................	158	32
Albany Railway...................................	528	75

Stone, Brick, Cement, Sand, etc.

Johnson & Wilson....................	256	00
Johnson & Wilson..................................	512	00
Wasson & Martin..................................	87	88
Howe's Cave Association............................	405	64
John Switzer......................................	244	43
T. S. Coolidge....................................	107	91
Peter McCabe.....................................	86	40
Peter McCabe.....................................	221	04
James C. Moore...................................	377	98
G. A. Sherwood...................................	4,655	30
F. G. Clark.......................................	2,424	75

Iron Work, Iron, Steel, Hardware, Tools, Steam Fittings, Plumbing, etc.

Sullivan & Ehlers.................................	5,000	00
Sullivan & Ehlers..	928	70
Sullivan & Ehlers.................................	9	66
Sullivan & Ehlers.................................	547	53
Sullivan & Ehlers.................................	18	95
Sullivan & Ehlers.................................	10	74
Breslin Bros...... ..:	27	05
M. Delehanty & Son...............................	1,591	83
Corning & Co.....................................	617	93
Bates & Johnson..................................	3,086	04
A. Van Allen, Jr..................................	3	24
Sullivan & Ehlers.'................................	3	14
Sullivan & Ehlers.................................	59	87
Sullivan & Ehlers.................................	680	65
Sullivan & Ehlers.................................	1,645	60

Lumber.

J. O. Towner & Co.................................	587	51
Thomas Murphy...................................	438	13

South-east Staircase.

James Sinclair & Co................................ $15,000 00

*Sundries — Paints, Oils, Rope, Upholstering, Covering and Decorating
Walls, etc.*

R. B. Wing..	$114	05
J. & J. Doran.....................................	3	50
D. W. Fonda & Co.................................	312	02
S. P. Templeton..................................	8	00
Simon Bell.......................................	15	50
Gorstendorfer Bros...............................	21	50
I. G. Perry......................................	26	36
John Mullon......................................	21	60
John G. Myers....................................	216	00
Commercial Telephone Co..........................	995	00
Fred. Beck.......................................	3,444	30

Total for September, 1884..................... $134,989 54

RECAPITULATION OF MONTHLY PAYMENTS.

October,	1883.................................	$185,789	83
November,	1883.................................	110,813	54
December,	1883.................................	108,342	70
January,	1884.................................	66,185	50
February,	1884.................................	3,523	61
March,	1884.................................	67,529	14
April,	1884.................................	129,425	61
May,	1884,................................	133,622	71
June,	1884.................................	121,173	72
July,	1884.................................	125,121	84
August,	1884.................................	119,307	56
September,	1884.................................	134,989	54

Total payments for fiscal year................... $1,305,825 30

TRANSFER

OF

SECURITIES FOR THE INSURANCE DEPARTMENT.

In pursuance of chapter 732 of the Laws of 1868, which provides as follows:

SECTION 1. No transfer of stocks, bonds and mortgages, or other securities, now held or hereafter received by the Superintendent of the Insurance Department under the provisions of any act authorizing deposits in the said Department, shall be deemed valid, or of binding force or effect, unless the same be countersigned by the Treasurer of the State, or in his absence from his office or inability to perform the duties of his office, by his deputy.

It shall be the duty of the Treasurer aforesaid to keep in his office, or in the office of the Superintendent of the Insurance Department, a book in which shall be entered the name of the company from whose accounts such transfer of securities is made by the Superintendent, and the name of the party to whom such transfer is made, unless such transfer shall be made in blank; and the par value of any stock so transferred shall be entered therein, and the amount for which every mortgage transferred is held by the Superintendent, and the name of the party to whom assigned, shall also be therein entered; and it shall be the duty of the Treasurer, immediately upon counter-signing and entering the same, to advise, by mail, the company from whose accounts such transfer is made of the kind of security and the amount of the same thus transferred.

§ 2. The Treasurer shall present in his annual report to the Legislature the total amount of such transfers or assignments countersigned by him.

The following is a statement of such transfers from the 1st of October, 1883, to the 30th of September, 1884:

* TRANSFER OF STOCKS.

Date.	From what company and to whom assigned.	Amount.
1883.		
Oct. 3.	From Sun Fire Office Co., of London, to Geo. B. McClellan and others, trustees.................	$100,000 00
5.	From Standard Fire Ins. Co., of N. Y., to same company.........	78,000 00
29.	From Sun Fire Office Co., of London, to Geo. B. McClellan and others, trustees.................	40,000 00
Nov. 5.	From Hamburg Magdeling Fire Ins. Co., to Superintendent Insurance Department, in trust for American Steam Boiler Ins. Co...............	100,000 00
5.	From Hamburg Magdeling Fire Ins. Co., ———..	100,000 00
Dec. 7.	From Sun Fire Office Co., of London, to Fiske & Hatch, N. Y.........	100,000 00
1884.		
Jan. 11.	From Sun Fire Office Co., of London, to Geo. B. McClellan and others, trustees.................	100,000 00
30.	From Sun Fire Office Co., of London, to Geo. B. McClellan and others, trustees.....	120,000 00
Feb. 4.	From British American Assurance Co., of Toronto, to same...............................	20,000 00
8.	From Sun Fire Office Co., of London, to Geo. B. McClellan and others, trustees.	30,000 00
8.	Lloyd's Plate Glass Ins. Co., of N. Y., to same....	23,000 00
14.	From Sun Fire Office Co., of London, to George B. McClellan and others, trustees.	120,000 00
March 4.	From Sun Fire Office Co., of London, to George B. McClellan and others, trustees	30,000 00
6.	From Lloyd's Plate Glass Ins. Co., N. Y., to same..	18,000 00
28.	From Provident Sav. Life Assur. Soc. of N. Y., to First Nat. Bank, N. Y. City.....	100,000 00
April 21.	From Sun Fire Office Co., of London, to George B. McClellan and others, trustees..........	50,000 00
23.	From Lloyd's Plate Glass Ins. Co., of N. Y., to Secretary of Treasury	50,000 00
May 13.	From Lloyd's Plate Glass Ins. Co., of N. Y., to same,	5,000 00
June 10.	From No. Amer. Life Ins. Co., of N. Y., to ———.	20,800 00
16.	From Accident Ins. Co., of North America, Montreal, to Secretary of Treasury.................	100,000 00
July 16.	From Liverpool, London and Globe Ins. Co. to Robert B. Mintern and others, trustees............	300,000 00
16.	From Universal Life Ins. Co., to Nathan D. Wendell, Receiver of same.	64,200 00
16.	From Continental Life Ins. Co., of N. Y., to A. B. Hepburn, Receiver of same	81,950 00
16.	From Knickerbocker Life Ins. Co., of N. Y., to Charles H. Russell, Receiver of same...........	86,250 00
18.	From Lion Life Ins. Co., of London, to Messrs. Plock & Co., N. Y.	50,000 00
26.	From Globe Mutual Life Ins. Co. of N. Y., to Alden S. Swan, Receiver of same....................	100,000 00

* Held in trust, for the companies named, by the Superintendent of the Insurance Department and by him transferred.

July 26. From Atlantic Mutual Life Ins. Co., of Albany, to
Edward Newcomb, Receiver of same.......... $100,000 00
28. From Guarantee Co., of North America, Montreal,
to Secretary of Treasury........... .... 200,000 00
Sept. 22. From La Confiance Ins. Co., of Paris, France, to
————— 50,000 00

Total transfer of stocks............................. $2,337,200 00

*Transfer of Bonds and Mortgages.

Date.	*From what company and to whom assigned.*	Amount.
1883.		
Nov. 1.	From Metropolitan Life Ins. Co. of N. Y., to same,	$7,000 00
1884.		
Jan. 9.	From Western N. Y. Life Ins. Co., to same, to Wm. Smyth, acting Superintendent.................	2,500 00
March 12.	From Sun Fire Office Co., of London, to George B. McClellan and others, trustees in United States, of Sun Fire Office Co...	40,000 00
April 21.	From Sun Fire Office Co., of London, to George B. McClellan and others, trustees.................	26,666 00
May 2.	From Western N. Y. Life Ins. Co., to satisfaction of mortgage.............................	5,000 00
July 16.	From Universal N. Y. Life Ins. Co., to Nathan D. Wendell, Receiver of same...................	5,000 00
22.	From Western N. Y. Life Ins. Co., Batavia, to O. C. Parker and D. W. Tomlinson, as joint Receivers of same..	5,000 00
22.	From Same to Same	5,000 00
	From Same to Same....	800 00
	From Same to Same.........................	1,074 00
	From Same to Same..........................	5,000 00
	From Same to Same.........................	1,000 00
	From Same to Same..........................	4,000 00
	From Same to Same..........................	2,850 00
	From Same to Same..........................	4,500 00
	From Same to Same	1,300 00
	From Same to Same	1,200 00

Total transfer of bonds and mortgages................. $117,890 00

Bank Department.

A provision similar to that for countersigning transfers of securities held by the Superintendent of the Insurance Department is made, by chapter 103 of the Laws of 1857, to apply to securities held by the Superintendent of the Bank Department.

The following is a statement of the transfers of such securities, between the 1st of October, 1883, and the 30th of September, 1884.

Transfer of Stocks for the Bank Department.

Date.	*From what bank transferred and to whom assigned.*	Amount.
1883.		
Nov. 8.	From North River Bank of New York to same	$4,000 00
8.	From Saratoga County Bank of Waterford to same.	4,000 00

* Held in trust, for the companies named, by the Superintendent of the Insurance Department and by him transferred.

Dec.	4.	From Home Bank of New York to same.........	$1,000.00
	4.	From Metropolitan Trust Co. to same.......	100,000 00
	10.	From American Loan and Trust Co. to same......	80,000 00
	17.	From Buffalo Loan, Trust and Safe Deposit Co. to same........	85,000 00
1884.			
Jan.	24.	From Randall Bank of Cortland Village to J. Howard King, President.....................	5,000 00
	24.	From same to same........ ····	6,000 00
	31.	From City Bank of Schenectady to ——.	5,000 00
April	8.	From Bank of Worcester to Secretary of the U. S. Treasury	1,000 00
June	12.	From Baldwin's Bank of Penn Yan to Secretary of Treasury	1,000 00
July	16.	From United States Trust Co. to United States Trust Co., N. Y. city....	200,000 00
	25.	From Union Trust Co. to Secretary of the Treasury.	100,000 00
	25.	From Exchange Bank of Clayton to Secretary of the Treasury.................................	1,000 00
		Total transfer of bonds and mortgages...............	$494,000 00

TRANSFER OF BOND AND MORTGAGES.

Date.		*From what bank transferred and to whom assigned.*	Amount.
1884.			
Jan.	25.	From Randall Bank to W. R. Randall............ ..	$2,500 00
		From Randall Bank to W. R. Randall...........	1,800 00
		From Randall Bank to W. R. Randall, discharged.	4,600 00
		From Randall Bank to W. R. Randall, discharged.	4,900 00
		From Randall Bank to W. R. Randall, discharged.	5,000 00
Sept.	9.	From Buffalo Loan, Trust & Safe Deposit Co. to same....	4,000 00
		Same to Same	2,000 00
		Same to Same	3,167 00
		Total transfer of bonds and mortgages	$27,967 00

Lightning Source UK Ltd.
Milton Keynes UK
UKHW020623201218
334296UK00006B/234/P